CELEBR ... YEARS
ZAGAT SURVEY

Back in 1979, we never imagined that an idea born during a wine-fueled dinner with friends would take us on an adventure that's lasted three decades – and counting.

The idea – that the collective opinions of avid consumers can be more accurate than the judgments of an individual critic – led to a hobby involving friends rating NYC restaurants. And that hobby grew into Zagat Survey, which today has over 350,000 participants worldwide weighing in on everything from airlines, bars, dining and golf to hotels, movies, shopping, tourist attractions and more.

By giving consumers a voice, we – and our surveyors – had unwittingly joined a revolution whose concepts (user-generated content, social networking) were largely unknown 30 years ago. However, those concepts caught fire with the rise of the Internet and have since transformed not only restaurant criticism but also virtually every aspect of the media, and we feel lucky to have been at the start of it all.

As we celebrate Zagat's 30th year, we'd like to thank everyone who has participated in our surveys. We've enjoyed hearing and sharing your frank opinions and look forward to doing so for many years to come. As we always say, our guides and online content are really "yours."

We'd also like to express our gratitude by supporting **Action Against Hunger,** an organization that works to meet the needs of the hungry in over 40 countries. To find out more, visit www.zagat.com/action.

Nina and Tim Zagat

ZAGAT®

CELEBRATING 30 YEARS

Cape Cod &
The Islands
Restaurants
2009/10

LOCAL EDITOR
Naomi Kooker
LOCAL COORDINATOR
Maryanne Muller
STAFF EDITOR
Bill Corsello

Published and distributed by
Zagat Survey, LLC
4 Columbus Circle
New York, NY 10019
T: 212.977.6000
E: capecod@zagat.com
www.zagat.com

ACKNOWLEDGMENTS

We thank Chris Decker, William DeSousa-Mauk, Nancy Gardella of the Martha's Vineyard Chamber of Commerce, Demaris Kooker, Jynell and Jeff Kristal of the Crocker House Inn, Dan Newcomb, Sara O'Reilly of Periwinkle Guest House, Christopher O'Reilly, Charlie Perkins, Steven Shukow and Darlene VanAlstyne, as well as the following members of our staff: Christina Livadiotis (assistant editor), Brian Albert, Sean Beachell, Maryanne Bertollo, Jane Chang, Sandy Cheng, Reni Chin, Larry Cohn, Alison Flick, Jeff Freier, Andrew Gelardi, Justin Hartung, Roy Jacob, Garth Johnston, Ashunta Joseph, Natalie Lebert, Mike Liao, Dave Makulec, Andre Pilette, Kimberly Rosado, Becky Ruthenburg, Jacqueline Wasilczyk, Sharon Yates, Anna Zappia and Kyle Zolner.

© 2009 Zagat Survey, LLC
ISBN-13: 978-1-60478-145-8
ISBN-10: 1-60478-145-9
Printed in the
United States of America

What's New

This year, Cape Cod and the Islands sadly bid farewell to a few beloved old-timers, which either ran their course or succumbed to the faltering economy. Among the departed are abbicci in Yarmouth Port, Clem & Ursie's in Provincetown and Restaurant 902 Main in South Yarmouth, plus yearlings Catch at the Terrace on Martha's Vineyard and Water Street on Nantucket. But at least one stalwart was saved from the chopping block: **Home Port,** the nearly 80-year-old shanty in Menemsha on the Vineyard, was bought in early 2009, and the new owners vow to keep it up and running just as it ever was.

VINEYARD VARIETY: A relatively high number of ventures opened on Martha's Vineyard this past year. **Sharky's Cantina,** a dirt-cheap Oak Bluffs Mexican, premiered part *dos* in Edgartown, where it joins fellow freshmen **Atlantic,** a casual, midpriced seafooder, and **Water St.,** serving pricey Eclectic cuisine in the upscale Harbor View Hotel & Resort. **Sidecar Café & Bar** offers inexpensive New England fare with Italian flair in Oak Bluffs, while Vineyard Haven welcomed two moderately priced options: Eclectic eatery **Salt Water** and American cafe and specialty-foods purveyor **Waterside Market.** Meanwhile, the Cape saw the premiere of only one notable newcomer, **Blackfish,** an upscale New American set in Truro's former Blacksmith Shop restaurant.

LIQUID ASSETS: Trend-watchers claim that a weak economy leads to stronger alcohol sales. That may explain why **Academy Ocean Grille** in Orleans, **Bramble Inn** in Brewster, **Sweet Life Café** in Oak Bluffs on the Vineyard and **Galley Beach** on Nantucket all underwent renovations that expanded or added bars.

DIAL IN: While some places follow the same schedule year-round, others have irregular seasonal hours and/or close for part or all of the winter. Call ahead before making a special trip.

Boston, MA
April 8, 2009

Naomi Kooker

Top Food Ratings

Excludes places with low votes. All restaurants are on Cape Cod unless otherwise indicated: M=Martha's Vineyard; N=Nantucket.

__28__ Company/Cauldron/N | *Amer.*

__27__ Inaho | *Japanese*
Topper's/N | *American*
Front St. | *Continental/Italian*
Pisces | *Med./Seafood*
Red Pheasant | *Amer./Fr.*
Bramble Inn | *American*
Chillingsworth | *French*
Abba | *Mediterranean/Thai*
Mews | *American*
Détente/M | *American*
Larsen's Fish/M | *Seafood*

__26__ 28 Atlantic | *Amer.*
Le Languedoc/N | *French*
Cape Sea Grille | *American*
Brewster Fish | *Seafood*
Bite/M | *Seafood*
Black-Eyed Susan's/N | *Amer.*
L'Étoile/M | *French*
Cafe Edwige/at Night | *Amer.*
L'Alouette | *French*

__25__ Atria/M | *American*
Regatta of Cotuit* | *American*
Sweet Life/M | *American*
Straight Wharf/N | *Seafood*

Lambert's Cove/M | *Amer.*
Nauset Beach Club | *Italian*
Beach Plum/M | *American*
Ocean House | *American*
Bleu | *French*
Catch of the Day* | *Seafood*
La Cucina Sul Mare* | *Italian*
Outermost Inn*/M | *American*
American Seasons/N | *Amer.*
Net Result/M | *Seafood*
Naked Oyster | *Seafood*
Belfry Inne | *American*
Sushi by Yoshi/N | *Japanese*
Chanticleer/N | *French*
Five Bays Bistro* | *American*
Queequeg's/N | *Eclectic*

__24__ Wicked Oyster | *Amer./Sea.*
Sir Cricket's | *Seafood*
Art Cliff Diner/M | *Diner*
HannaH's Fusion | *Asian Fusion*
Òran Mór/N | *Eclectic*
Terra Luna | *American*
Ships Inn/N | *Cal./French*
Devon's | *American/French*
Blue Moon Bistro | *Med.*

---

* Indicates a tie with restaurant above

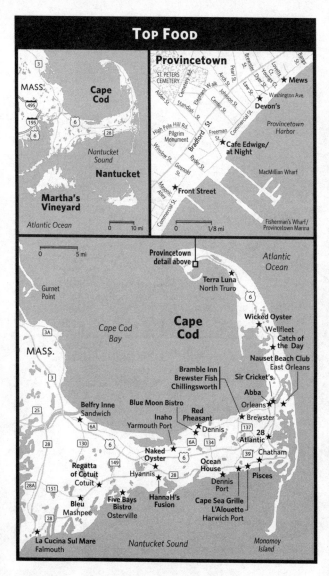

TOP FOOD

Cape Cod

MASS.

Cape Cod

Nantucket Sound

Nantucket

Martha's Vineyard

Atlantic Ocean

0   10 mi

Provincetown

ST. PETERS CEMETERY

★ Mews

Washington Ave.

★ Devon's

Provincetown Harbor

Pilgrim Monument

★ Cafe Edwige/ at Night

MacMillian Wharf

★ Front Street

Fisherman's Wharf/ Provincetown Marina

0   1/8 mi

---

0   5 mi

Provincetown detail above

Atlantic Ocean

Terra Luna North Truro

Gurnet Point

Cape Cod Bay

Cape Cod

★ Wicked Oyster
Wellfleet
Catch of the Day ★

Nauset Beach Club East Orleans
Sir Cricket's ★

MASS.

Bramble Inn
Brewster Fish
Chillingsworth

Abba
Orleans ★

Blue Moon Bistro
Inaho
Yarmouth Port

Red Pheasant
★ Brewster
Dennis

28 Atlantic
Chatham

Belfry Inne
Sandwich

Naked Oyster
Hyannis

Ocean House
Dennis Port

Pisces

Regatta of Cotuit
Cotuit

Hannah's Fusion

Cape Sea Grille
L'Alouette
Harwich Port

Bleu
Mashpee

Five Bays Bistro
Osterville

La Cucina Sul Mare
Falmouth

Nantucket Sound

Monomoy Island

Visit ZAGAT.mobi from your mobile phone

5

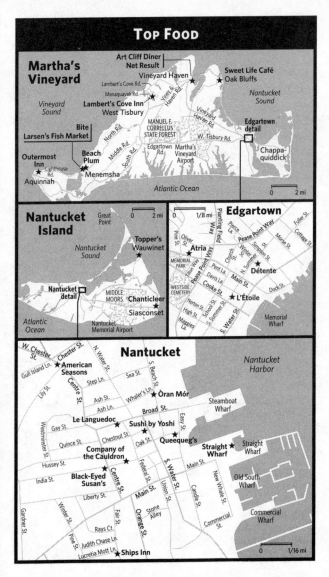

TOP FOOD

Martha's Vineyard

Art Cliff Diner
Net Result
★ Vineyard Haven

Sweet Life Café
★ Oak Bluffs

Lambert's Cove Rd.
Manaquayak Rd.
Lambert's Cove Inn
West Tisbury

Vineyard Sound

Vines & Haven Rds.

North Rd.

MANUEL F. CORRELLUS STATE FOREST

Vineyard Haven Rd.

Nantucket Sound

Edgartown detail ★

W. Tisbury Rd.

Edgartown Rd.
Martha's Vineyard Airport

Chappa-quiddick

Bite
Larsen's Fish Market

Middle Rd.
South Rd.

Beach Plum ★

Outermost Inn
Lighthouse Rd.
Aquinnah

Menemsha

Atlantic Ocean

0   2 mi

Nantucket Island

Great Point

0   2 mi

Nantucket Sound

Topper's ★
Wauwinet

Nantucket detail

MIDDLE MOORS

Chanticleer ★
Siasconset

Atlantic Ocean

Nantucket Memorial Airport

Edgartown

0   1/8 mi

Planting Field Way

Pierce La.
Oliver St.
Pine St.

Pease Point Way

Fuller St.
Cottage St.
Morse St.

Church St.
Winter St.
N. Summer St.
Simpson St.

Atria ★

Pent La.
Davis La.

Main St.

Détente ★

Cooke St.

WESTSIDE CEMETERY

Norton St.
School St.
Summer St.

L'Étoile ★

High St.

S. Water St.

Maggies La.

Dock St.

Memorial Wharf

MEMORIAL PARK

Nantucket

W. Chester St.
Chester St.
Gull Island Ln.

American Seasons ★

Nantucket Harbor

Centre St.
Lily St.
Step Ln.
Sea St.
N. Water St.
S. Beach St.

Òran Mór ★

Whaler's Ln.

Ash St.
Ash Ln.
Broad St.

Steamboat Wharf

Gay St.

Le Languedoc ★

Sushi by Yoshi ★

Easy St.

Westminster St.

Quince St.
Chestnut St.
Oak St.

Queequeg's ★

Straight ★ Wharf

Straight Wharf

Company of the Cauldron ★

Hussey St.

Federal St.
S. Water St.

New Whale St.

Old South Wharf

India St.

Black-Eyed Susan's ★

Centre St.

Main St.

Union St.

Candle St.

Gardner St.

Liberty St.

Orange St.

Stone Alley

Commercial St.

Commercial Wharf

Winter St.
Fair St.
Pine St.

Rays Ct.
Judith Chase Ln.
Lucretia Mott Ln.

Ships Inn ★

0   1/16 mi

Menus, photos, voting and more - free at ZAGAT.com

Ratings & Symbols

Zagat Top Spot	Name	Symbols	Cuisine	Zagat Ratings			
				FOOD	DECOR	SERVICE	COST

Area, Address & Contact

🔲 Tim & Nina's ◐ *Seafood* ▽ 19 | 15 | 18 | $15

Hyannis | 1½ Main St. (Second Ave.) | 508-555-1234 | www.zagat.com

Review, surveyor comments in quotes

"Even the Kennedys" make the "annual pilgrimage" to this Hyannis "seafood mecca", braving "agonizing" queues for "creamy clam chowda" and "all the usual fried suspects"; though the edifice "puts the 'shack'" in "'ramshackle'", picnic tables outside prove a "tranquil" retreat.

Ratings   **Food, Decor** and **Service** are rated on the Zagat 0 to 30 scale.

0 – 9	poor to fair
10 – 15	fair to good
16 – 19	good to very good
20 – 25	very good to excellent
26 – 30	extraordinary to perfection
▽	low response	less reliable

Cost   Our surveyors' estimated price of a dinner with one drink and tip. Lunch is usually 25 to 30% less. At prix fixe–only places we show the charge for the lowest-priced menu plus 30%. For unrated **newcomers** or **write-ins,** the price range is shown as follows:

I	$25 and below	E	$41 to $65
M	$26 to $40	VE	$66 or more

Symbols

🔲	highest ratings, popularity and importance
◐	serves after 11 PM
🅂	closed on Sunday
🅜	closed on Monday
⊄	no credit cards accepted

| | FOOD | DECOR | SERVICE | COST |

Cape Cod

☑ Abba *Mediterranean/Thai*

| | 27 | 21 | 24 | $54 |

Orleans | 89 Old Colony Way (bet. Old Tote & West Rds.) | 508-255-8144 |
www.abbarestaurant.com

For "scrumptious" flavors you "won't come across anywhere else", hit
this "old house" in Orleans where chef Erez Pinhas creates an "imaginative culinary fusion" of Med and Thai cuisines, which is "beautifully
presented" (along with a "superb wine list") by "knowledgeable" servers; insiders warn that "long waits, even with reservations", and "high
prices" are unavoidable, but the "cramped" interior can be skipped for
the "quieter, more spacious" deck.

Academy Ocean Grille Ⓜ *Eclectic/Seafood*

| | 22 | 19 | 20 | $45 |

Orleans | 2 Academy Pl. (Orleans Rd.) | 508-240-1585 |
www.academyoceangrille.com

"New owners" have "updated the decor" and "enlarged the bar" at this
"small", "relaxed" Eclectic seafooder in Orleans, but it remains a
"charming spot for an intimate dinner" (the patio is especially "great"
in summer", while a fireplace keeps it "cozy" in winter); better still, the
"competently served", "fresh" fare comes at "a decent price."

Adrian's *American/Italian*

| | ▽ 16 | 13 | 17 | $34 |

North Truro | Outer Reach Resort | 535 Rte. 6 (near Pilgrim Heights) |
508-487-4360 | www.adriansrestaurant.com

"Great views" of the bay are the real draw at this "casual", "family-friendly" North Truro eatery doling out American breakfasts and Italian
dinners – which may be "ordinary" at best ("please update the menu")
but at least feature "fine pizzas"; the interior "lacks charm", but the deck
is a "nice experience" (at "sunset" in particular) "if it's not too buggy."

Alberto's Ristorante *Italian*

| | 20 | 19 | 20 | $41 |

Hyannis | 360 Main St. (Barnstable Rd.) | 508-778-1770 | www.albertos.net
Tourists and locals alike "count on" – and get – "satisfaction" from everything they order off the "wide-ranging menu" at this longtime
Hyannis Northern Italian boasting a "romantic", "elegant" interior and
sidewalk cafe; whippersnappers protest it "needs a youth movement"
but "early birds" are too busy digging into their "bargain" "sunset dinners" to pay them any mind.

	FOOD	DECOR	SERVICE	COST

Amari Bar & Ristorante *Italian*

| 22 | 21 | 21 | $34 |

East Sandwich | 674 Rte. 6A (Jones Ln.) | 508-375-0011 |
www.amarirestaurant.com

"Generous portions" of "hearty red-sauce Italian" "like grammie used
to make" (at prices she would love) "draw quite a crowd" to this "rustic" East Sandwich eatery, "even during the long winter"; fans forgive
that the "huge", fireplace-blessed setting can get "way too noisy", in-
stead letting themselves be soothed by live music Friday and
Saturday; P.S. "you don't want to forget that reservation."

Anthony's Cummaquid Inn Ⓜ *Continental*

| 18 | 18 | 18 | $41 |

Yarmouth Port | 2 Main St./Rte. 6A (Willow St.) | 508-362-4501 |
www.pier4.com

The location makes this "large" Yarmouth Port Continental a "tourist haven", as the "views of the bay" are "second to none", especially if you
"get there before sunset"; though many find everything "enjoyable", old-
timers who "remember what the name used to mean" deem it a "shame"
that the decor's so "dated" and the fare "merely mediocre."

Aqua Grille *American/Seafood*

| 19 | 19 | 20 | $36 |

Sandwich | 14 Gallo Rd. (Town Neck Rd.) | 508-888-8889 |
www.aquagrille.com

A "favorite" for "sunny lunches", this Sandwich "standby" proffers
"reliable, tasty", midpriced New American seafood in "nonstressful"
surroundings featuring a "great bar" and "interesting views of the
Cape Cod Canal"; dinners are also "pleasant", especially with the increased likelihood that the "friendly service" won't be "slow."

Ardeo *Mediterranean*

| 20 | 17 | 20 | $28 |

South Yarmouth | Union Plaza | 23 Whites Path (Station Ave.) | 508-760-1500
Ardeo Grille at Kings Way *Mediterranean*
Yarmouth Port | 81 Kings Circuit (Oak Glen) | 508-362-7730
Ardeo on Main *Mediterranean*
Hyannis | 644 Main St. (Sea St.) | 508-790-1115
Ardeo Tuscan Tavern *Mediterranean*
Brewster | 280 Underpass Rd. (Independence Way) | 508-896-4200
www.ardeocapecod.com

"Reasonable prices" for a "wide selection" of "well-flavored"
Mediterranean dishes with "Middle Eastern accents" – "innovative

pizzas" being the highlight – keep this "unpretentious" Cape mini-chain "busy" with "families and large groups"; "efficient", "friendly staffs" help to make everyone feel "welcome" when they arrive and "delighted" when they leave.

Arnold's Lobster & Clam Bar ⊘ *Seafood* | 23 | 14 | 14 | $28 |

Eastham | 3580 Rte. 6 (Nauset Rd.) | 508-255-2575 | www.arnoldsrestaurant.com

"Be prepared to wait in line" for the "ultimate fried seafood experience" at this "no-frills", cash-only "clam shack" in Eastham, also known for a "super-fresh raw bar" and "awesome hot lobster rolls"; with ice cream, alcohol and miniature golf also on-site, it's easy to see how the annual "must-do" "family" "tradition" can get so "expensive."

Barley Neck Inn Dining Room *American* | 20 | 20 | 18 | $40 |

East Orleans | Barley Neck Inn | 5 Beach Rd. (bet. Barley Neck Rd. & Main St.) | 508-255-0212 | www.barleyneck.com

Housed in a former sea captain's manor, this "reliable" New American offers a "fresh"-seafood-focused menu in several "elegant", "romantic" rooms, one of which includes a fireplace for winter dining; adjoining is Joe's Beach Road Bar & Grille, a more "casual" "place for a quick bite to eat", drinks and weekend live music.

Baxter's Boathouse *New England/Seafood* | 18 | 16 | 15 | $28 |

Hyannis | 177 Pleasant St. (South St.) | 508-775-4490 | www.baxterscapecod.com

"You can't beat the views" at this seasonal "old-school" New England "boaters' hangout" on Hyannis Harbor, the site of "tourists" "rubbing elbows with salty" locals inside (home of a Thursday–Saturday night piano bar) or on the deck, where plates of "greasy"-"great" fried seafood must often be shielded from "pesky gulls"; though dollar-watchers calculate it's "overpriced" for what it is, even they make the "annual visit."

Bayside Betsy's *American* | 15 | 15 | 17 | $31 |

Provincetown | 177 Commercial St. (Winthrop St.) | 508-487-6566 | www.baysidebetsys.com

"Lovely" harbor views are "the best part" of this "campy, cute" "P-town fixture" offering a "scene-y bar" and "good enough" all-day New American fare at "reasonable prices"; "it's jammed in the summer with tourists", so the "wait for a table can be long" and

"Greenland might melt before you're served", but "Betsy herself is charming", and a little of that goes a long way.

Bee-Hive Tavern *American*
| 19 | 20 | 20 | $30 |

East Sandwich | 406 Rte. 6A (bet. Atkins Rd. & Jacobs Meadow) | 508-833-1184

Valued by visitors as a convenient "stop for lunch when driving home from the Cape" and by locals as an "efficient" "alternative" year-round, this "bee-themed" American cottage in East Sandwich emits "country charm" thanks in part to a "friendly staff"; the "relaxed" mood is bolstered by fare that, while vacillating between "average" and "very good", does the trick for reasonably priced "comfort."

Belfry Inne & Bistro Ⓜ *American*
| 25 | 26 | 22 | $50 |

Sandwich | Belfry Inne | 8 Jarves St. (bet. Main St. & Rte. 6A) | 508-888-8550 | www.belfryinn.com

Adorned with stained-glass windows and other "elegant" "remnants" from its past as a church, this "enchanting" Sandwich bistro is a "real find" for "clever, tasty" and wholly "divine" New American dishes; "saintly service" and live weekend jazz piano are two more blessings – just be prepared to dig deep when the basket is passed; N.B. a more casual lunch is available in the adjoining Painted Lady cafe.

Betsy's Diner *Diner*
| 18 | 19 | 18 | $19 |

Falmouth | 457 Main St. (bet. King St. & Lantern Ln.) | 508-540-0060

"If you're nostalgic for the '50s", this Falmouth diner is "the place to go" for American comfort food served by a "chatty staff" in "authentic" retro environs; "tourists line up for the dynamite breakfast", but lunch and dinner are equally "fun" – albeit possibly "not so good for the arteries" ("the 'eat heavy' sign outside says it all").

Bistro at Crowne Pointe *American*
| 22 | 21 | 22 | $50 |

Provincetown | Crowne Pointe Historic Inn & Spa | 82 Bradford St. (Prince St.) | 508-487-6767 | www.crownepointe.com

"Quiet, romantic" dinners are the stock in trade of this "intimate" Provincetown bistro boasting "charming" High Victorian decor and "amazing views", not to mention "inventive, attractively presented" New American fare; "polite, skillful service" and an "impressive wine list" complete the "memorable" (and somewhat pricey) picture; N.B. lunch available for guests of the Crowne Pointe Historic Inn & Spa only.

	FOOD	DECOR	SERVICE	COST

NEW Blackfish ⓜ American
| 24 | 23 | 21 | $49 |

Truro | 17 Truro Center Rd. (Castle Rd.) | 508-349-3399

"Bravo" to this "classy" Truro addition proffering a "creative" "combination of rich, gourmet" New American fare and "knockout" "fresh" seafood in the former Blacksmith Shop restaurant decked out with brick walls, copper-top tables and a concrete bar; while many feel the service "could be more attentive" for such "upscale" pricing, that doesn't stop it from being "packed with tourists" (those in-the-know say "go on a weeknight" for less "noise").

Bleu French
| 25 | 21 | 21 | $43 |

Mashpee | Mashpee Commons | 10 Market St. (North St.) | 508-539-7907 | www.bleurestaurant.com

Though "set in a Mashpee Commons storefront", Francophiles deem dining at this "lively" "change of pace for Cape Cod" is "almost like being in France", as it offers "authentic bistro" fare (alongside some "novel" yet equally "satisfying" "seasonal" preparations) and "a bit of attitude"; the "cozy" setting – swathed in multiple shades of blue – has an "urbane" feel that matches the slightly "pricey" dinner tabs (lunch is a relative "bargain").

Blue Moon Bistro ❶ Mediterranean
| 24 | 20 | 22 | $40 |

Dennis | 605 Main St./6A (New Boston Rd.) | 508-385-7100 | www.bluemoonbistro.net

Despite its "small, simple" setting, this "real gem" in historic Dennis shines with "superb" Mediterranean meals that are only "a little expensive"; the "nice people" who operate it make "whole families" feel welcome, and they in turn "love it year-round", especially before performances at the nearby Cape Cod Center for the Arts.

Bookstore & Restaurant Seafood
| 19 | 15 | 16 | $34 |

Wellfleet | 50 Kendrick Ave. (Commercial St.) | 508-349-3154 | www.wellfleetoyster.com

"Talk about fresh and sweet!" – the oysters are just-harvested at this "reliable standby" for "value" seafood in Wellfleet (the menu's broad, but your best bet is to "stick to the basics"); if "long waits", "old-time-everything" decor and service that can seem "uncaring" rankle, hit the patio or second-floor deck and get lost in the "wonderful" harbor views or a volume from the attached tome-seller.

	FOOD	DECOR	SERVICE	COST

⎘ Bramble Inn Ⓜ American
27 | 25 | 27 | $65

Brewster | Bramble Inn | 2019 Main St./Rte. 6A (bet. Breakwater Rd. & Crocker Ln.) | 508-896-7644 | www.brambleinn.com

"An amazing experience" awaits in this "charming" 1861 Brewster farmhouse where "absolutely fabulous, innovative but not precious" New American "works of art" are ferried by "outstanding" servers in four "quaint, elegant" Victorian dining rooms "enhanced" by a "beautiful new bar"; "superb wines" can turn "pricey" tabs into "wallet-busters", but they're "worth it" for such a "special night out."

Brazilian Grill Brazilian
21 | 16 | 19 | $37

Hyannis | 680 Main St. (bet. Sea & Stevens Sts.) | 508-771-0109

"Vegans beware!" – though there's a "fine salad bar" at this "upbeat", reasonably priced Brazilian rodizio in Hyannis, it's hard to escape "solicitous" staffers who are so "efficient in their singular task: bringing you piles and piles" of "succulent" grilled meats; indeed, you'll have to "beg them to stop" – and "you'll be so disappointed" when they do (for best results, "don't eat for a week" beforehand).

⎘ Brewster Fish House Seafood
26 | 18 | 23 | $47

Brewster | 2208 Main St./Rte. 6A (Stonehenge Dr.) | 508-896-7867

An "annoying no-reservations policy" that leads to nearly "intolerable waits" makes getting into this "tiny" Brewster venue a "pain in the neck", but "it's all worth it in the end" for "perfectly prepared" seafood sprinkled with "mouthwatering" "nouvelle twists" and complemented by a "strong wine list"; it may "look like nothing" from the outside, but "unfailingly polite" staffers (not to mention "somewhat pricey" checks) help give it that fine-dining air.

Bubala's by the Bay Eclectic/Seafood
16 | 14 | 16 | $32

Provincetown | 183-85 Commercial St. (bet. Court & Winthrop Sts.) | 508-487-0773 | www.bubalas.com

Watching the "parade of beautiful men and their dogs down Commercial Street" from the "see-and-be-seen patio" is "the main event" at this P-town "standby" that also exhibits "great views of the bay" from the "air-conditioned interior"; indeed, the "vast", seafood-heavy Eclectic menu seems "marginal" (and often "a bit pricey") to the "busy" scene, which also trumps "uninspired" decor and servers who swing from "humorous" to "torturous."

| | | FOOD | DECOR | SERVICE | COST |

Buca's Tuscan Roadhouse *Italian*

`23` `21` `22` `$47`

Harwich | 4 Depot Rd. (Rte. 28) | 508-432-6900 | www.bucasroadhouse.com
You're in Harwich, but you "might as well be in Tuscany" when you sup
at this "charming" "gem" serving Northern Italian cuisine that's sometimes "traditional", sometimes "innovative" and always "superb"; the
"romantic" setting – marked by beamed ceilings, red-and-white-
checked tablecloths and a fireplace – feels even warmer thanks to a
"gracious", "knowledgeable" staff, and while it's a tad expensive, the
"excellent wine list" displays "fair prices."

Cafe Edwige/Edwige at Night *American*

`26` `17` `21` `$48`

Provincetown | 333 Commercial St. (bet. Freeman & Standish Sts.) |
508-487-2008 | www.edwigeatnight.com
"Wonderful breakfasts", "amazing brunches" and "creative", "care-
fully constructed" dinners complemented by "imaginative drinks"
command somewhat elevated prices at this "bustling" second-floor
Provincetown New American employing an "accommodating" staff,
the "snug", "funky" setting offers "no ocean view or special atmosphere", but the wooden "booths by the window are great for people-
watching – if not a little hard on the backside."

Cape Sea Grille *American*

`26` `24` `23` `$50`

Harwich Port | 31 Sea St. (Rte. 28) | 508-432-4745 | www.capeseagrille.com
At this "elegant" Harwich Port seasider, the "superb attention to
detail" extends from the "sophisticated" New American cuisine
(starring "refreshing takes on Cape Cod favorites", "perfectly paired"
with a "superb wine list") to the "idyllic setting" in an "old sea captain's house" and the "winning", "well-paced" service; for the "perfect
special occasion", insiders say "ask for the porch" – and bring a
mass of moolah.

Captain Frosty's *New England/Seafood*

`21` `10` `16` `$18`

Dennis | 219 Main St./Rte. 6A (S. Yarmouth Rd.) | 508-385-8548 |
www.captainfrosty.com
"A Cape Cod vacation isn't complete without a drive" to this Dennis
"throwback" clam shack where fried New England seafood "cravings"
(there are also "great lobster rolls", burgers, etc.) are sated with "over-
flowing" portions and for "reasonable prices"; it's what "memories are
made of", especially if you "save room" for "soft-swirl ice cream."

	FOOD	DECOR	SERVICE	COST

Captain Kidd, The *Pub Food*
18 **20** **20** **$28**

Woods Hole | 77 Water St. (Luscombe Ave.) | 508-548-8563 |
www.thecaptainkidd.com

"Beautiful views of quaint Eel Pond", "friendly service" and moderate
prices make this nautically themed Woods Hole "charmer" a "nice"
choice "while waiting for the ferry to Martha's Vineyard"; the pub food
is "tasty" enough, if "nothing fancy", while the deck's "great in summer", the interior's "cozy in winter" and the whole enterprise is "fun
for kids" always.

Captain Linnell House Ⓜ *American*
22 **25** **23** **$53**

Orleans | 137 Skaket Beach Rd. (West Rd.) | 508-255-3400 |
www.linnell.com

"Dress up" without feeling "out of place" at this "elegant" "old sea
captain's" "mansion" in Orleans, where "experienced servers" present
a "varied menu" of Traditional American fare "with flair" in "classy"
French neo-classic dining rooms that overlook sprawling lawns; since
this is the kind of "costly" "evening you save for", "romance"-seekers
urge you come "without the kids" – "please!"

Captain Parker's Pub *New England*
18 **14** **18** **$26**

West Yarmouth | 668 Rte. 28 (W. Yarmouth Rd.) | 508-771-4266 |
www.captainparkers.com

Connoisseurs "put up with" often long "waits" for the "exceptional",
"thick and creamy" clam chowder for which this "homey", "rustic"
(and possibly "long in the tooth") West Yarmouth "destination" is "fa-
mous"; many feel the rest of the New England fare is purely "pass-
able", though on the upside, it's "moderately priced."

Casino Wharf *Italian/Seafood*
∇ **20** **21** **21** **$48**

Falmouth | 286 Grand Ave. (bet. Dartmouth Ct. & Falmouth Heights Rd.) |
508-540-6160 | www.casinowharffx.com

"Spectacular views of Vineyard Sound", especially "on the deck
overlooking the beach", create a "lovely" backdrop at this
Falmouth Heights venture offering "solid" Northern Italian
seafood and pasta; it can get "noisy" with chatter and live entertainment (nightly in-season, Friday and Saturday off), but if you
"go as a couple", the "elegant" environs can help to make
the evening romantic.

	FOOD	DECOR	SERVICE	COST

Catch of the Day *Seafood* | 25 | 13 | 22 | $29 |

Wellfleet | 975 Rte. 6 (Marconi Beach Rd.) | 508-349-9090 | www.wellfleetcatch.com

Wellfleet day-trippers expecting "standard clam-shack" fare at this "unpretentious" market discover "quite a find" in seafood that's not only "fresh, fresh, fresh" but "perfectly prepared" and "value" priced to boot; a "pleasant staff", wine and beer make it "great for a nice lunch" on premises, but "don't overlook takeout" for a picnic at a nearby beach.

Chapoquoit Grill *American* | 22 | 15 | 20 | $34 |

West Falmouth | 410 W. Falmouth Hwy./Rte. 28A (Brick Kiln Rd.) | 508-540-7794 | www.chapoquoitgrill.com

"Don't be fooled" by the "ordinary" setting of this West Falmouth "mainstay" – the wood-fired brick-oven pizzas are "spectacular" and the rest of the "creative" New American dinners are what "you would expect at a more upscale restaurant" (and an "excellent value" too); "throngs of people, especially in summer", keep it perpetually "lively" – and make waits for tables often "lengthy."

Chart Room *New England/Seafood* | 20 | 18 | 18 | $36 |

Cataumet | 1 Shipyard Ln. (Shore Rd.) | 508-563-5350

Many Cataumet summerers make this "old-timer" a "weekly" "ritual", creating "a mob scene" where the waits for tables and for the "predictable" but "tasty" New England seafood take "forever"; no matter, they just cool their heels with "deadly but delicious mudslides" while listening to the "lively entertainment" and taking in the "beautiful sunset" and "magical" harbor views; P.S. the "to-die-for lobster sandwich" is "not on the menu", but "everyone orders it."

Chatham Bars Inn *American* | 22 | 26 | 23 | $55 |

Chatham | Chatham Bars Inn | 297 Shore Rd. (bet. Chatham Bars Ave. & Seaview St.) | 508-945-0096 | www.chathambarsinn.com

You half "expect to bump into Gatsby" at this "absolutely elegant" oceanside Chatham "luxury hotel" with "several great" eateries, starting with an "airy" main room filled with "old-world charm" and a "dressy crowd" supping on "imaginative" New American fare "well prepared and presented" by "attentive" servers; "less fancy" but still generally "splendid" are the tavern and the beach grill, the latter boasting "amazing views"; all venues, meanwhile, command "premium prices."

	FOOD	DECOR	SERVICE	COST

Chatham Squire *Eclectic* | 18 | 14 | 18 | $29 |

Chatham | 487 Main St. (bet. Chatham Bars Ave. & Seaview St.) | 508-945-0945 | www.thesquire.com

"Townies and tourists" "mingle easily" at this "informal" "Chatham institution" with a "family-friendly" "restaurant side" doling out "basic pub fare" and Eclectic entrees "at decent prices" and a "terrific" "tavern side" "bustling" with "overwhelming crowds" (expect "huge waits" in season); the setting – festooned with a "colorful" collection of license plates – is "outdated on purpose", but thankfully, "cool and shady in the summer and warm and cozy in the winter."

◪ Chillingsworth Ⓜ *French* | 27 | 26 | 26 | $73 |

Brewster | 2449 Main St./Rte. 6A (Foster Rd.) | 508-896-3640 | www.chillingsworth.com

For "grand events", Brewster bigwigs choose this "formal" "heaven" set on a "charming" 300-year-old estate where the "sensational" chef-owner "injects New England flair" into "glorious" New French prix fixes, which are then conveyed by "graceful" servers in "romantic rooms"; though said splurgers say it's "worth every penny", the hoi polloi would rather hit the "more laid-back" adjacent bistro for the same "excellence" offered à la carte at "a fraction of the price."

Circadia Bistro *American* | ▽ 23 | 18 | 19 | $49 |

Harwich Port | 86 Sisson Rd. (Gilbert Ln.) | 508-432-2769 | www.circadiabistro.com

"Outstanding" New American cuisine "prepared with the skills associated with good French cooking" and "friendly service" shine at this Harwich Port venue, a "lovely" 1830s Cape Cod country house whose "formal" dining room seems "more Colonial inn" to some (and just plain "dated" to others); "for lower-priced", "lighter" fare, try the "cozy" tavern side whose fireplace provides an especially "warm welcome during the bleak winter."

Ciro & Sal's *Italian* | 20 | 18 | 16 | $41 |

Provincetown | 4 Kiley Ct. (Commercial St.) | 508-487-6444 | www.ciroandsals.com

"Part of the fabric of the Cape" for more than 50 years, this "P-town perennial" still delivers "reliable", "no-nonsense" Northern Italian fare in a "cutesy" yet "cramped" "below-street-level" dining room with

FOOD | DECOR | SERVICE | COST

hanging Chianti bottles; it can be "romantic" ("if there aren't too many loud parties"), "especially next to the fireplace in winter", but during the high season, when service becomes "erratic", many locals would just as soon leave the "dark dungeon" to the "tourists."

Clancy's of Dennisport *American*

22 | 18 | 21 | $30

Dennisport | 8 Upper County Rd. (bet. Rtes. 134 & 28) | 508-394-6661 | www.clancysrestaurant.com

Clancy's Fish 'n Chips & Beach Bar *American*

Dennisport | 228 Lower County Rd. (Shad Hole Rd.) | 508-394-6900 | www.clancysfishnchips.com

"Be prepared to wait" for "hours" "during the summer" for this Dennisport duo "popular" with "locals" and "knowledgeable tourists" requiring a "typical Cape Cod menu" with "value" (the American "burgers, sandwiches and seafood" are sold in "portions big enough to share"); there's a "great view of the river" at the Upper County Road locale, but both offer "screened-in" "outdoor dining", not to mention "friendly" staffers.

Cobie's Clam Shack ⊘ *Seafood*

19 | 7 | 12 | $18

Brewster | 3260 Main St. (Linnell Landing Rd.) | 508-896-7021 | www.cobies.com

Folks with a "hankering for seafood" wax "nostalgic" when they pedal up to this "self-serve" stand "on the bike trail near Nickerson State Park" in Brewster, a "summer stop" since 1948 for fried clams, lobster rolls, chowder, ice cream and more, all served in "good portion sizes for the money"; it may be "no better or worse than similar joints", but for an "in-the-rough" experience, it "hits the spot."

Cooke's Seafood *Seafood*

- | - | - | I

Orleans | 1 S. Orleans Rd. (Rte. 28) (Rte. 6A) | 508-255-5518
Hyannis | 1120 Iyannough Rd. (Rte. 132) (Bearses Way) | 508-775-0450
Mashpee | 7 Ryans Way (Great Neck Rd.) | 508-477-9595
www.cookesseafood.com

For more than 30 years, this Orleans landmark – which has spun off locales in Hyannis and Mashpee – has stood as an inexpensive yellow beacon to seafoodies craving whole-belly fried clams, lobster rolls and other fish fixes; after getting their fare from the counter, guests either settle into the dining room, which is festooned with Cape-themed paintings, eat under an awning on the patio or take it back to the beach.

Coonamessett Inn *American*

18	20	20	$37

Falmouth | Coonamessett Inn | 311 Gifford St. (Jones Rd.) | 508-548-2300 | www.capecodrestaurants.org

"An older crowd tends" to spend "nicer occasions" at this "charming" Falmouth "institution" offering "old-school" American fare that, while "not very inspiring", is "well prepared" and conveyed by an "attentive, experienced staff" (Sunday brunch in particular is "great"); their grandkids, though, regard it as a bit of a "stuffy" "function farm", marveling "it's not 1959 anymore, but you'd never know it" were it not "for the prices."

Dan'l Webster Inn *American*

20	22	21	$44

Sandwich | Dan'l Webster Inn | 149 Main St. (Rte. 130) | 508-888-3622 | www.danlwebsterinn.com

Whether in the "expensive, elegant" main room, the "less-expensive", "warm and cozy tavern" or the "light and airy" botanical conservatory, patrons enjoy the "old Colonial charm" of this Sandwich "institution" – serving "modestly ambitious, well-executed" New American fare – just as they have for "over 30 years"; but since it's almost "exactly the same" as it ever was, modish types would rather "leave it to the blue hairs."

Devon's *American/French*

24	20	22	$50

Provincetown | 401½ Commercial St. (Washington Ave.) | 508-487-4773 | www.devons.org

"Organic and seasonal" ingredients pepper the "inventive", "refined" New American–French menu proffered at this "charming" all-day "Cape Cod beach cottage" in Provincetown, where "Devon himself" ensures that the service stays "warm" and "attentive"; "prices are high", but they're "worth every penny" assure admirers who also appreciate that the "wine list complements the food so well."

Dolphin *Seafood*

21	17	21	$46

Barnstable | 3250 Main St./Rte. 6A (Hyannis Rd.) | 508-362-6610 | www.thedolphinrestaurant.com

This Barnstable "townie bar" adequately sates "families", "judges and lawyers" who desire "nothing fancy" in their "fresh seafood" and Traditional American dishes, but do require "reliability" and "friendly" service; the decor may be somewhat "tired", but sitting "by the fire on a chilly night" is as "cozy as can be."

	FOOD	DECOR	SERVICE	COST

Dunbar Tea Room *British/Tearoom* — 22 | 22 | 20 | $26

Sandwich | Dunbar Tea Shop | 1 Water St. (Main St.) | 508-833-2485 |
www.dunbarteashop.com

"You swear you're in the English countryside" when you come upon
this "wonderful little" carriage house "in the heart of old Sandwich
Village" vending "high-tea lunch choices" ("satisfying" sandwiches,
"baked goods to die for") amid "elegant", "pristine" and, natch, "fem-
inine decor"; just "come at an off-hour if you don't want a long wait"
and "slow" service.

Enzo *French* — ∇ 24 | 20 | 23 | $53

Provincetown | Enzo Guest House | 186 Commercial St. (Court St.) |
508-487-7555 | www.enzolives.com

Formerly serving Italian, this "charming" Victorian guest-house restaurant in Provincetown has recently "revised" its menu to feature "varied,
interesting" and ultimately "fabulous" French Provençal dishes, about
which the "friendly", "knowledgeable" servers can advise; what hasn't
changed are the "lovely, intimate" rooms and the "street-level terrace",
which offers "great" views of the "flamboyant traffic passing by."

Fairway Restaurant & Pizzeria *American* — 18 | 14 | 19 | $26

North Eastham | 4295 State Hwy./Rte. 6 (Brackett Rd.) | 508-255-3893 |
www.fairwaycapecod.com

In the morning, "great breakfasts" are served alongside "the best gos-
sip" in town to "North Eastham's finest" at this "friendly, family-run"
"coffee shop"; in the evenings, its bar is a "fun place" to "watch the
Sox", while the booths host groups chowing down on American grub –
it may be "so-so", but there's "loads of it", providing "top value for
your buck"; N.B. no lunch.

Fanizzi's by the Sea *American/Italian* — 20 | 21 | 21 | $32

Provincetown | 539 Commercial St. (Kendall Ln.) | 508-487-1964 |
www.fanizzisrestaurant.com

Like "being in a houseboat at high tide" with "water lapping at the window", this "casual" Provincetown East Ender that "juts out into the
bay" is "popular with locals" who find its "reasonable" American-
Italian seafood "dependably good" ("just not distinctive") and the
staff "always nice"; "one of the few places" "open year-round", it's
even more appreciated as a "cozy" "off-season resource."

	FOOD	DECOR	SERVICE	COST

Fazio's Trattoria *Italian*

| 20 | 15 | 15 | $36 |

Hyannis | 294 Main St. (Center St.) | 508-775-9400 | www.fazio.net

Fans feel this "cozy", "basic" Hyannis Italian "doesn't get the attention it deserves" for its "homemade pastas", "fantastic pizzas" and "great breads", all of which are "not too expensive"; but perhaps that's because some customers only "used to recommend it" – currently, they can't stop "fuming" over the "indifferent service" and "terrible acoustics."

Finely JP's *American*

| 21 | 18 | 20 | $40 |

Wellfleet | 554 Rte. 6 (Castanga Dr.) | 508-349-7500

Whether they find the New American cuisine created at this Wellfleet year-rounder "super" or "marginal", or the service "personable" or "not worth mentioning", "customers always seem happy" that "the price is right"; the "modern room", deck and parking bear "no hassles."

Firefly Woodfire Grill & Bar ❿ *Eclectic*

| 20 | 17 | 16 | $36 |

Falmouth | 271 Main St. (Shore St.) | 508-548-7953 | www.fireflywoodfiregrill.com

Large, "nice crowds" fill this Falmouth "fun spot" for "good people-watching" from the "cute tables on the sidewalk" and the "chic bar" scene; as for sustenance, some just come for "pizza and drinks" because the rest of the "extensive variety" of "adequate" Eclectic fare may be "too expensive for what you get"; peace-seekers, meanwhile, "avoid it" altogether due to the "excessive noise."

Fishmonger's Cafe *American/Seafood*

| 18 | 19 | 18 | $35 |

Woods Hole | 56 Water St. (Luscombe Ave.) | 508-540-5376

"Its days as a hippie enclave are a distant memory" applaud supporters of this all-day New American in "quaint Woods Hole", where new owners have made "creative" "improvements" to the menu (more seafood and Mediterranean accents, "less sprouts"); unfortunately, foes are "disappointed" that the "unexciting" fare doesn't fully complement the "friendly service" and "terrific water views."

Five Bays Bistro *American*

| 25 | 20 | 22 | $50 |

Osterville | 825 Main St. (Wianno Ave.) | 508-420-5559 | www.fivebaysbistro.com

"Stylish", "upscale" Ostervilleans "meet and greet" at the "active bar" of this "dynamite" New American with a "warm, contemporary setting" and "friendly" service; if the dining area is on your agenda ("reservations are necessary"), be prepared to "yell across the table to converse" – or just "wear earplugs", focus your attention on the "plate-licking good" victuals and be proud that you can "afford it."

Friendly Fisherman's Seafood   ▽ 24 | 12 | 16 | $21
North Eastham | 4580 Rte. 6 (Oak Rd.) | 508-255-6770

"Be careful" or "you'll drive by this little fish market" in North Eastham, a mecca for "large", "wonderful lobster rolls" and "ultrafresh" fried seafood, also doled out in "huge portions"; so what if there's "no atmosphere"? – it's "convenient" for "trips to the National Seashore", "less touristy than others" and quite a BYO "deal."

✓ Front Street Continental/Italian   27 | 20 | 24 | $49
Provincetown | 230 Commercial St. (Masonic Pl.) | 508-487-9715 | www.frontstreetrestaurant.com

"You can't go wrong" with anything off the "delicious, gourmet" Continental *carte*, the "extensive" Italian menu (starring "expertly made favorites") or the "awesome wine list" at this "expensive" Provincetown two-for-one with "faultless service" and a "cavelike" yet "romantic" "windowless" setting in a Victorian house; "be sure to make advance reservations", because space is tight and it's "always packed."

Gina's by the Sea 🅜 Italian   21 | 16 | 21 | $39
Dennis | 134 Taunton Ave. (Chapin Beach Rd.) | 508-385-3213 | www.ginasbythesea.com

Dennis locals think "tourists are usually unable to find this" "fun, funky" "hole-in-the-wall Italian" – but it's "worth trying", if not for a "taste of Old Cape Cod" ("average" though it may be), then at least "for its character and for the characters who work there"; just "get there early, as it's already jammed by 6 PM."

Gracie's Table 🅜 Spanish   23 | 19 | 23 | $42
Dennis | 800 Main St./Rte. 6A (Scargo Hill Rd.) | 508-385-5600 | www.graciestablecapecod.com

"Tired of fish?" – "excite your taste buds" with the "many wonderful flavors" found in the Spanish (particularly Basque) tapas "nicely presented" at this "solid establishment" near Dennis' Cape Playhouse; the colorfully decorated, bi-level space can sometimes feel "cramped"

	FOOD	DECOR	SERVICE	COST

ith parties letting the "interesting cocktails" flow freely while "order-
ig several things to share" ("hence driving the price up").

HannaH's Fusion Bar & Bistro *Asian Fusion* | 24 | 20 | 22 | $41 |

yannis | 615 Main St. (Sea St.) | 508-778-5565 | www.hannahsbistro.com

Different from most things on the Cape", this "solid player" in Hyannis
as "highly skilled hands" fashioning a "wide variety" of "inventive",
delicious" and "beautifully presented" Asian fusion fare; "urban-
endy" design features (clean lines, low lighting), a happening bar
ith a "nice wine list" and "fancy" pricing add to the "city" feeling.

Heather *American* | - | - | - | E |

Mashpee | South Cape Village | 20 Joy St. (bet. Charles St. & Donna's Ln.) |
08-539-0025 | www.restaurantheather.com

urprise, surprise – hidden inside the South Cape Village shopping
enter in Mashpee is this bustling dinner-only New American that
onors the seasons with a menu featuring local seafood and innova-
ve dishes; the venue is separated into a candlelit dining room with
ablecloths, mesquite floors and walls adorned with local artists'
aintings and a patio for summertime alfresco dining.

Hemisphere *New England* | ▽ 17 | 19 | 19 | $33 |

andwich | 98 Town Neck Rd. (Freeman Ave.) | 508-888-6166 |
ww.hemispherecapecod.com

we-inspiring views" of "Cape Cod Bay and the canal" create return-
es to this beach-themed Sandwich New Englander, especially since
ey feel just as "comfortable dressing up [to dine] inside" as they do
sitting on the deck in shorts sipping a cocktail"; indeed, the atmo-
phere "more than makes up for" times when the "standard fish house
are" dips from "solid" to "unfortunate."

mpudent Oyster *Seafood* | 23 | 18 | 21 | $42 |

hatham | 15 Chatham Bars Ave. (Main St.) | 508-945-3545

Whether you opt for the "sunny upstairs room" or the "noisy", "cozy
ar" with "mussels and a glass of wine" at this "fun", "friendly", "fix-
are" in "charming Chatham", you're guaranteed "high-quality" sea-
ood in "fantastic combinations"; dinner prices are geared to the
ffluent", while "lunch is a better deal", and it's especially "great off
eason, since you have to make a reservation well in advance to get in
uring the summer."

☑ Inaho Ⓢ *Japanese*

27 | 20 | 20 | $42

Yarmouth Port | 157 Main St./Rte. 6A (Summers St.) | 508-362-5522 |
www.inahocapecod.com

"Right on target" cheer maki mavens of this Yarmouth Port Japanese
and its "perfectly prepared", "totally terrific" sushi and "innovative
delicious specials", all of which easily "surpass the decor", as there's
"a tight fit between tables" that necessitates "pulling in every time" a
staffer passes (some of them are "slow" and "sullen"); meals here can be
"expensive", but they're "worth it" – and "cheaper than flying to Tokyo".

Island Merchant ❂ *American/Caribbean*

– | – | – | M

Hyannis | 302 Main St. (bet. Barnstable Rd. & Center St.) | 508-771-1337 |
www.theislandmerchant.com

Have a "fun" island experience right in Hyannis at this "tiny place" dis-
playing an "interesting", moderately priced Caribbean-flecked New
American menu, fake palm trees and bright colors; "music lovers" dig
the live acts on most evenings, cinephiles on a budget come for
$2-burger movie nights in the winter, while everyone raises their
glasses to the "great rum punch and other drinks" served at all times.

JT's Seafood *Seafood*

17 | 13 | 15 | $29

Brewster | 2689 Main St./Rte. 6A (Winslow Landing Rd.) | 508-896-3355 |
www.jt-seafood.com

The promise of "right-off-the-boat" seafood followed by ice cream in-
cites "huge lines" of "families" at "all times of the day" at this
"cafeteria-style" clam shack in Brewster; the window workers do their
best to be "quick and efficient", and while some numbers-crunchers
calculate it's a "good value for the money", others deem it too "expensive" for such "ordinary" eats.

Karoo Kafe *S African*

▽ 24 | 18 | 19 | $18

Provincetown | 338 Commercial St. (Center St.) | 508-487-6630 |
www.karookafe.com

Ready to try "wild boar sausage, ostrich burgers or snail rangoon"?
then slide into this eatery where the "different-for-the-area" South
African fare is "well prepared" and "inexpensive", the latter another
"rarity in P-town"; adventurers say the "small indoor/outdoor" digs' bold
colors and art lend it an exotic feel, and the "friendly" staff helps to ren-
der it "always a good choice", particularly for "quick", "casual lunches".

	FOOD	DECOR	SERVICE	COST

Kate's Seafood ⚅Ⓜ *Seafood* ▽ 20 | 9 | 16 | $19

Brewster | 285 Paines Creek Rd. (bet. Lower Rd. & Main St./Rte. 6A) | 508-896-9517

"The sign saying 'fried seafood, ice cream' tells all you need to know" about this inexpensive "roadside clam shack" in Brewster, which dispenses its "great" 'n' "greasy" goods (featuring "iconic onion blossoms") via "window service" to "families" at "picnic tables"; some sweet-toothed surveyors "only go" for the "many flavors" of cold cones, which they take "to the beach at Paine's Creek to watch the sunset."

La Cucina Sul Mare *Italian* 25 | 18 | 22 | $40

Falmouth | 237 Main St. (Walker St.) | 508-548-5600 | www.lacucinasulmare.com

"Roll up your sleeves" before digging into the "huge portions" of "traditional Italian" fare "beautifully prepared" at this Falmouth "jewel" where a "husband-and-wife team (he's in the kitchen)" directs a "strong staff"; the "small" interior and "great patio" get quite "crowded", leading to "long waits on summer weekends", but if you can "be patient", perhaps with "a drink at the bar", "you won't be let down."

L'Alouette *French* 26 | 20 | 25 | $49

Harwich Port | 787 Main St./Rte. 28 (Julien Rd.) | 508-430-0405 | www.lalouettebistro.com

"Don't expect to diet" at this Harwich Port "gem", as its "superb" "French" fare is classically "rich – but worth the calorie splurge" (and the "Cape prices"); excitement-seekers are "put off" by the "standard white-tablecloth" decor ("designed for an older crowd" *peut-être?*), but even they appreciate that the "tables are not on top of each other", not to mention the "lovely service" and "top-notch wine list."

Landfall *Seafood* 18 | 21 | 19 | $36

Woods Hole | 2 Luscombe Ave. (Water St.) | 508-548-1758 | www.woodshole.com/landfall

"Watching the Martha's Vineyard ferries coming and going" while dining on "simply grilled" (some say "predictable") seafood has been a "family tradition" since 1946 at this "lively" Woods Hole seafood "standby" with a somewhat "kitschy" "nautical"-themed dining room and a deck "overlooking the harbor"; but tipplers who only come to "relax with a beer" think it's now "better known for its bar scene."

	FOOD	DECOR	SERVICE	COST

Laura & Tony's Kitchen *American*

| − | − | − | I |

North Eastham | Blue Dolphin Inn | 5950 Rte. 6 (Nauset Rd.) | 508-240-6096 | www.lauraandtonyskitchen.com

North Easthamers "really can't beat" the "all-you-can-eat" breakfasts laid out at this funky, "relaxing" American, "especially at the price": under $10; the "gracious owners" also operate a catering service.

Laureen's *Eclectic*

| ∇ 23 | 19 | 19 | $29 |

Falmouth | 170 Main St. (Townhall Sq.) | 508-540-9104 | www.laureensrestaurant.com

"Falmouth's version of a chick flick" could be filmed at this "charming, bistro-style" cafe with an airy, arty atmosphere and an "interesting" Eclectic menu that stars "wonderful" pastries for breakfast, "gourmet sandwiches" for lunch and "creative Middle Eastern" and Mediterranean fare for dinner; "friendly service" lets diners relax in the "quaint" dining room or "people-watch" from the "cute outdoor tables."

Liam's at Nauset Beach *Seafood*

| 20 | 9 | 13 | $19 |

East Orleans | 239 Beach Rd. (Surf Path) | 508-255-3474

"Onion ring heaven" ("possibly the best" ever) can be found at this "ramshackle shed" on an East Orleans sand dune, also serving "fried fish and ice cream" that can be taken to "funky" "picnic tables" or back to your blanket; critics carp about paying relatively "costly" tabs and "waiting in long lines for ordinary takeout", but "when you're at Nauset Beach, there's no better place – in fact, there's no other place."

Lobster Pot *Eclectic/Seafood*

| 22 | 17 | 20 | $38 |

Provincetown | 321 Commercial St. (Standish St.) | 508-487-0842 | www.ptownlobsterpot.com

The "slightly downtrodden exterior" (look for the "neon sign") "belies" the "delicious lobsters" that "just come so easily out of their shells", plus Eclectic "takes on traditional seafood dishes" (all only "slightly above market prices") at this P-Town "tourist landmark"; the bi-level space is a real "madhouse in summer", so "prepare to wait", hope to "get a window" for "amazing views" and "pray for nice people to be seated around you", as "they will be really close."

	FOOD	DECOR	SERVICE	COST

Lorraine's *Mexican*
▽ 20 | 16 | 15 | $38

Provincetown | 133 Commercial St. (Pleasant St.) | 508-487-6074 | www.lorrainesrestaurant.vpweb.com

Everyone agrees this "small, dark, no-frills" Provincetown Mexican set in a teak-and-mahogany edifice boasts an "amazing tequila selection", from which "margaritas that don't skimp" are made; while surveyors split on the suppers ("superb" vs. "lacking distinct flavors") and service ("friendly" vs. "dreadful"), they concur once more about the question of reservations: make them or risk an "interminable wait."

Mac's Seafood Market & Grill *Seafood*
24 | 15 | 17 | $30

Wellfleet | 265 Commercial St. (Kendrick Ave.) | 508-349-0404

Mac's Shack *Seafood*

Wellfleet | 91 Commercial St. (Railroad Ave.) | 508-349-6333 www.macsseafood.com

Proof that "you can't judge a book by it's cover", these "plain" Wellfleet fisheries "expertly prepare" "just-out-of-the-ocean" seafood ("not all fried!") and "generous ice cream scoops", plus "unusual selections" like "wonderful sushi" and burritos; at the beachside grill, "you stand in line, order, they call your number and you eat at picnic tables in the sand" (ideally during an "astounding sunset"), while the roadside-shack sibling offers interior dining as well as a patio.

Marshside, The *Seafood*
15 | 25 | 17 | $33

Dennis | 28 Bridge St. (Sesuit Neck Rd.) | 508-385-4010 | www.themarshside.com

"Bright, cheerful", "spacious" and "spectacular" are some of the accolades raining down on this longtime seafood purveyor's "great new building", which still boasts "gorgeous views" of the East Dennis marsh; now, patrons suggest, "rebuild the menu" of "nondescript" fare (it's "rather pricey" too), train the "inexperienced" members of the staff and "take reservations" (as it stands, you can "expect long waits at the bar or on the porch outside").

Mews *American*
27 | 25 | 25 | $54

Provincetown | 429 Commercial St. (Lovetts Ct.) | 508-487-1500 | www.mews.com

"Life doesn't get any better" than at this year-rounder in P-town's East End, where "upbeat", "refined" staffers make "right-on recommendations" about the "divine" New American fare (the "chef does wonderful things with fresh, local ingredients"); the "more elegant", "romantic" downstairs dining room boasts "million-dollar views" of the bay, while the "lively" upstairs cafe is a place to enjoy "cheaper choices" and an "out-of-this-world vodka selection" with "a group of friends"; P.S. "make reservations way in advance."

Misaki *Japanese*   ▽ 24 | 14 | 16 | $31

Hyannis | 379 W. Main St. (Pitchers Way) | 508-771-3771 | www.misakisushi.com

"While it doesn't look like much on the outside" (or inside for that matter), this Japanese joint in Hyannis employs "skilled sushi chefs" whose "top-notch" creations exhibit pure "artistry", and at "reasonable prices" no less; though complaints about "off-putting" staffers abound, there are early reports that new owners have introduced "friendlier", more "efficient" service.

Moby Dick's *New England/Seafood*   23 | 14 | 17 | $27

Wellfleet | 3225 Rte. 6 (Gull Pond Rd.) | 508-349-9795 | www.mobydicksrestaurant.com

It "looks like a tourist trap", but this "high-quality", "nautical"-themed Wellfleet "institution" turns out "gigantic portions" of "all the usual" seafood suspects at "moderate prices" (BYO makes it even "easier on the wallet"); the lines that lead to its "odd but effective hybrid" of counter and (picnic) table service are "beyond ridiculous", but it's "worth every minute" – and "you'll think about it all winter."

Naked Oyster Bistro & Raw Bar *Seafood*   25 | 19 | 22 | $47

Hyannis | 20 Independence Dr. (Rte. 132) | 508-778-6500 | www.nakedoyster.com

"If you're looking for 'typical Cape', go someplace else", since this "upscale" "gem" "tucked away" in a Hyannis strip mall maintains a "happening", "modern setting" (mahogany accents, handcrafted, shell-shaped light fixtures) to present its "sophisticated menu" of "exquisite" seafood, which is "served up by a courteous staff"; "don't expect bargains", but do count on "a wait in season" if you didn't "call for reservations" first.

	FOOD	DECOR	SERVICE	COST

Napi's Eclectic
19 | 20 | 18 | $38

Provincetown | 7 Freeman St. (Bradford St.) | 508-487-1145 |
www.napis-restaurant.com

This "funky institution on a backstreet in Provincetown" is "where locals go off-season" to get a little bit of "everything, from Greek to Italian to Brazilian" ("great vegetarian choices" and "Portuguese specialties" too); "matching" the Eclectic menu is the "quirky", art-strewn decor – it may be "over the top", but it's got real "character"; P.S. there's "free parking", "no small benefit" in these parts.

Nauset Beach Club Italian
25 | 21 | 22 | $52

East Orleans | 222 Main St. (Beach Rd.) | 508-255-8547 |
www.nausetbeachclub.com

A "temple to Northern Italian cooking", this "high-end" East Orleans venture offers an "exciting menu" "prepared with imagination and flair", complemented by an "extensive wine list" and presented by "sincere, gracious" staffers; though its evokes its name with "earth tones" and wicker (it's "not a beach club"), some feel the setting's somewhat marred by being noisy", "dark" and "cramped" – but they're in the minority, as most attest to "top-notch experiences" all around.

⬛ Not Your Average Joe's American
18 | 16 | 18 | $26

Hyannis | Cape Cod Mall | 793 Iyannough Rd. (Airport Rd.) | 508-778-1424 |
www.notyouraveragejoes.com

"Fun for a night away from the stove", this "spirited" Hyannis outpost of the local chain and its "down-to-earth" staff serve up "reasonably priced" American comfort chow from an "enormous", "something-for-everyone" menu (be warned: its focaccia and dipping oil starter is "addictive" and "could be an entire meal"); picky eaters find it "out of the corporate playbook", but most label it "easy" for "solid" grazing.

Ocean House Ⓜ American
25 | 25 | 24 | $48

Dennisport | 425 Old Wharf Rd. (Depot St.) | 508-394-0700 |
www.oceanhouserestaurant.com

"Artfully prepared" New American cuisine with a "heavy Pan-Asian influence" served by a "professional, friendly" staff "always matches and usually exceeds" the "picture-perfect postcard view" of Nantucket Sound at this Dennisport "gem"; "even if you only go for appetizers" and "fantastic drinks" at the "happening bar", "it's worth the visit" –

just try to arrive before sunset, "bring someone you want to impress" (and plenty of cash) and "program the GPS so you don't get lost."

Optimist Café, The *American/British* ∇ 21 | 21 | 22 | $22

Yarmouth Port | 134 Rte. 6A (Clark Rd.) | 508-362-1024 |
www.optimistcafe.com

"What a delightful spot!" – this inexpensive American-British cafe set in an 1849 captain's residence in Yarmouth Port "lives up to its name" with gingerbread trim outside, "funky"/cheery interiors featuring works by local artists and "fun service"; "tasty" lunches and high tea offer a "nice break from typical Cape fare", while "little girls" swoon over "wonderful breakfast" fare like heart-shaped waffles.

Orleans Inn *American* 17 | 17 | 19 | $38

Orleans | Orleans Inn | 21 Rte. 6A (Orleans Rotary) | 508-255-2222 |
www.orleansinn.com

When dining at this renovated Victorian-cum-American inn eatery, the "porch in summer", with its "nice view of Orleans Town Cove", is "the place to be" (the interior's a bit "fuddy-duddy"); the eats are "pedestrian", but they're not too highly priced, so one "can see why families like it."

Osteria La Civetta *Italian* – | – | – | M

Falmouth | 133 Main St. (Post Office Rd.) | 508-540-1616 |
www.osterialacivetta.com

From the "pleasant", "rustic" setting to the "woman from Bologna" who owns and runs it to the "handmade pastas" and other "simple, exquisite" Northern Italian dishes, this "intimate" Falmouth storefront "feels and tastes authentic"; the portions are "not big" and prices run at a "slight premium", but it's "worth visiting" – and bringing home some imported meats and cheeses from the retail section too.

Oyster Company Raw Bar & Grill *Seafood* 23 | 17 | 21 | $35

Dennisport | 202 Depot St. (Rte. 28) | 508-398-4600 |
www.theoystercompany.com

"As one would expect from the name", the "raw bar is exceptional" at this "Cape Cod–casual" Dennisport "gem" ("the owners farm their own Quivet Neck oysters"), while the rest of the seafood menu is "creatively prepared" and "scrumptious", as are other items "for the burgers-and-beer crowd"; it's a "tourist favorite", but factor in "neighborly" service and "reasonable prices", and it's "clear" to see why "locals like it too."

Paddock *New England/Seafood*

| 20 | 19 | 20 | $40 |

Hyannis | West End Rotary | 20 Scudder Ave. (Main St.) | 508-775-7677 | www.paddockcapecod.com

"Pleasant" and "reliable", this "family-run" Hyannis haunt serves "tasty", slightly "pricey" New England seafood in "several different" "old-world" "fine dining" rooms (young 'uns peg them as "time warps"); its convenient location next to the Melody Tent makes it a "great stop before or after a concert", and while service might be a little "slow" at peak times, the "experienced" staff works to make "you feel like a VIP at all times."

☑ Pisces *Mediterranean/Seafood*

| 27 | 19 | 23 | $51 |

Chatham | 2653 Main St. (Forest Beach Rd.) | 508-432-4600 | www.piscesofchatham.com

"Just-caught seafood" with "imaginative", "flavorful" Mediterranean preparations is ferried by "friendly, knowledgeable" servers at this "charming" Chatham "diamond"; the "intimate" "beach-chic", artwork-festooned setting gets "loud" and "crowded" (it "definitely requires reservations") and "prices are high", but for diehards, "weekends on the Cape aren't great" without an evening here.

Port, The *American/Seafood*

| 23 | 23 | 21 | $40 |

Harwich Port | 541 Main St./Rte. 28 (Sea St.) | 508-430-5410 | www.theportrestaurant.com

Things just "keep getting better" at this "modern, trendy restaurant in traditional Harwich Port", what with the addition of a "first-class" raw bar and "increased offerings" on the "creative", "sparkling" New American seafood menu; "a younger crowd" is as attracted to the "buzzy", "big-city" scene as it is to the "attractive", "efficient" staffers, even when some toss "a bit of 'tude."

Post Office Café ◐ *American*

| 16 | 12 | 14 | $27 |

Provincetown | 303 Commercial St. (Standish St.) | 508-487-3892

The "ordinary" American "diner fare" at this "bland" box is "priced at the lower end" for P-Town, but it's "nothing to write home about"; "all dishes" are delivered "with a side of staff attitude" (sometimes it's flat-out "disdainful"), but that and the "crowded, loud" and "chaotic" atmosphere is "just part of the experience."

| | FOOD | DECOR | SERVICE | COST |

Red Inn *New England*

| | 24 | 26 | 23 | $60 |

Provincetown | Red Inn | 15 Commercial St. (Province Lands Rd.) | 508-487-7334 | www.theredinn.com

"Enter through a delightful garden", start off with a "huge, delicious cocktail" "on the deck" while "looking out at the bay at sunset" ("breathtaking"), then settle in for "expertly prepared" (and "expensive") New England fare featuring "wonderful" local fish at this "class act" in an "incredible old hotel" nearly "on the tip of Provincetown"; "knowledgeable", "hospitable" service furthers its deserved reputation as a "sublime", "romantic getaway."

☑ Red Pheasant *American/French*

| | 27 | 24 | 25 | $53 |

Dennis | 905 Main St./Rte. 6A (Elm St.) | 508-385-2133 | www.redpheasantinn.com

Whether in summer when the "luscious gardens" "bloom" or "in the winter" "when the big fireplace is roaring", this "lovely antique" barn in Dennis provides a "special", "formal" setting for "gourmet" New American cuisine that "emphasizes seasonal" ingredients ("high-end seafood", "exceptionally prepared game") and "complex" French twists; "efficient" staffers and an "incredible wine list" are two more reasons why enthusiasts save up their dough to "go back over and over again."

Regatta of Cotuit at the Crocker House *American*

| | 25 | 23 | 24 | $57 |

Cotuit | 4631 Falmouth Rd./Rte. 28 (Rte. 130) | 508-428-5715 | www.regattaofcotuit.com

"Anyone who considers themselves a foodie will have an enjoyable evening" at this historic Federal mansion in Cotuit, as the New American fare is "interesting" and "memorable" (those who query some of the more "oddball combinations" depend on the "impeccable" servers – they really "know the menu"); "special-occasion" celebrators and "couples" laud it too, especially the seven "serene", "cozy" dining rooms – it's just "not a family place", least of all because of the "expense."

Roadhouse Cafe *Seafood/Steak*

| | 20 | 19 | 19 | $43 |

Hyannis | 488 South St. (Sea St.) | 508-775-2386 | www.roadhousecafe.com

"Escape" from "busy Hyannis" to this "convivial" hangout offering "lots of choices in terms of both" environments – which include "somewhat upscale" dining rooms, a "lighter-fare" bistro and a bar, all featuring wood paneling and nautical antiques – and "terrific" seafood and steaks served in "nice portions"; jazz on Mondays, a pianist on weekends and valet parking are "added bonuses."

RooBar *American*
21	20	21	$37

Chatham | 907 Main St. (bet. Heritage & Snow Lns.) | 508-945-9988
Falmouth | 285 Main St. (Cahoon Ct.) | 508-548-8600
www.theroobar.com

"Trendy comes to Cape Cod" in the form of these "noisy" "crowd-pleasers" with New American menus that offer "something to tickle any-one's taste" – and with everything from "$12 pizzas to $25 entrees", ev-ery budget to boot; expect "hopping bars" at both the Falmouth locale and the Chatham iteration, which boasts the bonus of a "covered patio."

Ross' Grill *American*
22	22	21	$44

Provincetown | 237 Commercial St. (bet. Gosnold St. & Masonic Pl.) |
508-487-8878 | www.rossgrillptown.com

"Comfortably chic" environs with "gorgeous views" of Provincetown Harbor create a "memorable" setting for "smart", "reliable" New American fare paired with "terrific" *vins* at this only "slightly higher priced" eatery/wine bar; repeat customers cheer the mostly "friendly" service and the fact that it "now takes reservations" – "a major plus for a place with an inevitable line and so few tables."

Scargo Café *American*
20	18	21	$35

Dennis | 799 Main St./Rte. 6A (bet. Corporation Rd. & Hope Ln.) |
508-385-8200 | www.scargocafe.com

"Catch dinner before the theater" or yuck it up with the "locals" over "a nightcap afterward" at this year-rounder "across from the Cape Playhouse" in Dennis serving "solid", "reasonably priced" ("albeit not particularly inventive") New American vittles; the "comfortable", woody space (dating from 1865) is "well-run" by two brothers who en-sure the staff provides a "friendly" greeting upon arrival, "a kind thank you when leaving" and "attentive" service in between.

Siena *Italian*
21	20	19	$38

Mashpee | Mashpee Commons | 38 Nathan Ellis Hwy. (Rte. 28) |
508-477-5929 | www.siena.us

Sating both the "spaghetti-and-meatballs crowd" and osso buco-cravers is never easy, but this "big, noisy" Mashpee Commons Italian with "nice outdoor seating" "deserves an A for effort": "if you want something, it's somewhere on the menu", and brought in "huge portions" for moderate prices to boot; indeed, "just about everyone" leaves "satisfied" – unless they're trying to catch a movie next door and they're stuck with a "spotty" server.

Sir Cricket's Fish & Chips ∅ *Seafood* — 24 | 8 | 19 | $18

Orleans | 38 Rt. 6A (Orleans Rd.) | 508-255-4453

There's "nothing fancy" at this "busy" Orleans spot – just "fabulous" "English-style fish 'n' chips" and other inexpensive, "excellent seafood from the store next door"; there's also "not much in terms of seating" (what there is resembles a "high-school cafeteria"), so do like the locals and get it to go.

Stir Crazy Ⓜ *Cambodian* — 23 | 16 | 20 | $28

Pocasset | 570 MacArthur Blvd., Rte. 28 (Portside Dr.) | 508-564-6464 | www.stircrazyrestaurant.com

"Gifted" chef-owner Bopha Samms serves up a "welcome change" – namely "delectable", "affordable" Cambodian cuisine with "fresh ingredients" and a "local twist" – just as she has for the past 20 years at her place in Pocasset; "generous but not overwhelming portions" are brought by "friendly" staffers in the pleasant digs, which feature authentic artwork and a bar.

Terra Luna *American* — 24 | 18 | 20 | $46

North Truro | 104 Shore Rd. (Windigo Ln.) | 508-487-1019

This "noteworthy" North Truro New American "feels like a neighborhood" "standard" thanks to a "casual", "rustic", "low-key setting" (the former site of a stagecoach stop) and an "interesting" "combo of seasonal specials and reliable" classics; it's "quite popular", but "small", so be sure to ask the "friendly" staffers for "a table with elbow room."

Trevi Café & Wine Bar *Mediterranean* — - | - | - | M

Mashpee | Mashpee Commons | 25 Market St. (Fountain St.) | 508-477-0055 | www.trevicafe.com

From the fountain at the front entrance to the awning-topped patio, this Mashpee venue exhibits European flair that extends to its mid-priced Mediterranean menu of tapas, pastas, panini and more; with hardwood floors and candlelight, the casual dining room is a romantic escape, while the granite bar is a place to get lost in television.

	FOOD	DECOR	SERVICE	COST

☑ Twenty-Eight Atlantic *American*

26	29	25	$65

Chatham | Wequassett Inn | 2173 Orleans Rd./Rte. 28 (Pleasant Bay Rd.) | 508-430-3000 | www.wequassett.com

You "must see" the "beautiful" decor and "phenomenal" view of Pleasant Bay at this all-day dining room in a "fancy" Chatham resort, but you also have to sample the New American cuisine, which often travels "beyond creative and delicious", all the way to "rapturous"; with "top-notch service" added to the mix, it's unsurprisingly "over-the-top expensive", but if you come "knowing what you're getting into", you'll "leave feeling elated."

Vining's Bistro *Eclectic*

▽ 24	17	24	$44

Chatham | Gallery Bldg. | 595 Main St. (Seaview St.) | 508-945-5033

"Leave your children home" before seeking out this "hard-to-find" second-floor bistro "overlooking Main Street" in Chatham, where the "casual" setting's as "understated" as the "sophisticated" Eclectic "menu offering a wealth of perfectly [wood-] grilled meats and seafood" is "adventurous"; the "friendly" staff also has an "excellent wine selection" on hand, adding to experiences that "never disappoint."

Whitman House Restaurant, The *American*

▽ 21	23	21	$36

Truro | 7 Great Hollow Rd. | 508-487-1740 | www.whitmanhouse.com

"Take your favorite aunt" for a "fantastic" meal at this "classy", "cozy" American set in an 1894 inn on four acres of landscaped grounds in Truro; run by the same family for more than four decades, the delightfully "old-fashioned" setting includes four Early American dining rooms as well as the more casual Bass Tavern.

Wicked Oyster *American/Seafood*

24	19	22	$43

Wellfleet | 50 Main St. (off Rte. 6) | 508-349-3455

"If it swims around the Cape, it's likely on the menu" (and "typically caught that day") at this "lively" New American in a "charming" early-1700s Wellfleet home providing "pleasant, prompt service" and "dazzlingly prepared", "deliciously wonderful" seafood-centric breakfasts, lunches and dinners (they're "great bangs for the buck" too); the "casual", "charming" room is "large", but so popular, "reservations are absolutely necessary in season."

	FOOD	DECOR	SERVICE	COST

Wild Goose Tavern *American* ▽ 21 | 21 | 21 | $35

Chatham | Chatham Wayside Inn | 512 Main St. (bet. Chatham Bars Ave. & Library Ln.) | 508-945-5590 | www.wildgoosetavern.com

A "great menu variety", featuring plenty of "pub-style" American fare, and "chipper service" draw "families" to this Chatham tavern, which pleasantly surprises moms and dads "expecting a hard hit to the wallet" with moderate prices; the "spacious" dining room "can be noisy" (good for when you want to "talk without being overheard"), while the bar is a "fun place" "to meet locals."

Winslow's Tavern *American* 20 | 21 | 18 | $38

Wellfleet | 316 Main St. (bet. Bank St. & Holbrook Ave.) | 508-349-6450 | www.winslowstavern.com

Wellfleet families find the "wonderful" New American fare, "affordable prices" and mostly "friendly service" "more than enough to warrant a return trip" to this "great old building", while oenophiles toast the "unique wine list", which they explore over "more casual meals" at the "upstairs bar"; "tables by the window overlooking the patio" are prized in the "white-all-over" main room, but "eating outside" may be best, since the "noise level" inside is "unbelievable."

Martha's Vineyard

Alchemy *American* 22 | 23 | 20 | $49

Edgartown | 71 Main St. (bet. School & Summer Sts.) | 508-627-9999

"Cosmopolitan ambiance" materializes at this "expensive" New American where "trendy pretty people" come "to be seen" in the "handsome" lounge upstairs (the milieu of "value bar snacks") and "lively bistro" downstairs, which features outdoor seating "overlooking the always interesting Edgartown streetscape"; the "solid, tasty" dishes and "great wines" keep it a "perennial favorite" for locals, except in January, when it's closed.

Art Cliff Diner *Diner* 24 | 17 | 21 | $18

Vineyard Haven | 39 Beach Rd. (Five Corners) | 508-693-1224

Some "island secret" – "impossibly long waits" prove the "dreamy crêpes", waffles and omelets are all-too-common knowledge at this "kitschy" "longtime tradition"; so drag yourself to Vineyard Haven "at

FOOD DECOR SERVICE COST

the crack of dawn" and "bring the paper" and a "bottle of champagne for mimosas", because "a trip to the Vineyard is not complete without breakfast" here; P.S. lunches are equally "fabulous" – and popular.

NEW Atlantic *Seafood*
| - | - | - | M |

Edgartown | 2 Main St. (Water St.) | 508-627-7001 | www.atlanticmv.com
"Young" cooks "turn out some fine fare" at this casual Edgartown seafooder with a midpriced menu focusing on fresh ingredients; owned by the same folks as the exclusive Boathouse club upstairs, the space maintains the feel of an upscale watering hole with white wainscoting and a marble bar, while exhibiting TV sports and harbor views.

Atria *American*
| 25 | 25 | 24 | $60 |

Edgartown | 137 Main St. (bet. Green & Pine Sts.) | 508-627-5850 | www.atriamv.com
"Clever combinations result in truly delicious dishes" at this "refreshingly different" Edgartown New American committed to "local, organic" ingredients, "impeccable service" and "expensive" tabs; a "Hollywood crowd" likes to be seen in the "exquisite", "sophisticated dining room", "romantic" types choose the "elegant", "candle-filled garden", while a nightcap in the "chic yet casual" cellar lounge is "highly recommended" to all.

Balance ⑤Ⓜ *American*
| ▽ 23 | 17 | 19 | $57 |

Oak Bluffs | 9 Oak Bluffs Ave. | 508-696-3000 | www.balancerestaurant.com
Critiques of this Oak Bluffs New American's cavernous "new space" are, unfortunately, not stellar: though it's "intended to be hip", it comes off as a "cheap cafeteria", with "loud, loud, loud" acoustics to match; regardless, the "generous" portions of "creative", somewhat pricey fare, which is ferried by "upbeat" staffers, keep many "coming back."

Beach Plum Inn *American*
| 25 | 26 | 26 | $61 |

Menemsha | Beach Plum Inn | 50 Beach Plum Ln. (North Rd.) | 508-645-9454 | www.beachpluminn.com
"Timed right, you'll see a beautiful sunset while eating expertly prepared", "inspired" New American cuisine plated like "mini architectural wonders" at this "secluded, serene" and "romantic retreat" with "gorgeous views" of Menemsha Harbor; "impeccable service" bolsters the feeling that you've been "invited to an elite dinner party" – although this one ends with a "pricey" bill (it's "worth it"); N.B. BYOB.

	FOOD	DECOR	SERVICE	COST

Bite, The ♥ *Seafood* — 26 | 11 | 17 | $20

Menemsha | 29 Basin Rd. (North Rd.) | 508-645-9239 |
www.thebitemenemsha.com

"It's fried seafood nirvana" at this cash-only take-out "shack with picnic tables crammed by the roadside" in Menemsha; though the "prices clearly reflect its status as a landmark", that doesn't stop clam-diggers from joining the "long lines" ("nothing to be intimidated by"), then taking the short walk to the beach for a "beautiful" "sunset picnic."

☑ Black Dog Tavern *American* — 19 | 18 | 18 | $33

Vineyard Haven | 20 Beach St. Ext. (Water St.) | 508-693-9223 |
www.theblackdog.com

"Crowds still line up" for "great breakfasts" and "worthy lunches" at this "casual" American "icon" "overlooking the gorgeous harbor" in Vineyard Haven; some say that "dinner is good too", just as many counter it's "unexciting", but either way, it's "not overly expensive", "fine for kids" and "you can advertise that you've eaten here" with "all manner of clothing and accessories with its ubiquitous" logo; N.B. BYOB.

Chesca's *Eclectic/Italian* — 23 | 22 | 23 | $52

Edgartown | 38 N. Water St. (Winter St.) | 508-627-1234

Edgartonians find it "hard to choose" from the selection of "well-prepared", "delicious" Italian-inspired Eclectic fare proffered at this "noisy" yet "fun night out", and though it's pricey, they deem it "reasonable for the quality and location"; "no reservations" for parties under six mean there's "always a wait", but it's easily dealt with by "sitting on the porch" with an "inventive cocktail" and "watching the crowds go by."

David Ryan's *American* — 15 | 16 | 16 | $36

Edgartown | 11 N. Water St. (Main St.) | 508-627-4100 |
www.davidryans.com

"Edgartown singles" advise "stick to the cocktails" and microbrews at this bi-level "prototypical tourist trap", because it's "much better for nightlife" than dining; that said, when you're "walking around town and in need of a comfortable" meal, the location is "convenient", while the American fare is "acceptable" (if "too salty") and moderately priced.

Z Détente *American*

27 **22** **24** **$69**

Edgartown | 3 Nevin Sq. | Winter St. (Water St.) | 508-627-8810 |
www.detentemv.com

It may just be wishful thinking when some surveyors opine that "not
everyone knows about" this "terrific", "tucked away" Edgartonian,
since you need to "make a reservation early" if you want to experience
chef Kevin Crowell's "adventurous", "awesome" New American creations and his wife Suzanna's "charming" hostessing skills; "service is
helpful without being obsequious", so whether you eat in the "pleasant" if "cramped" interior or the "small", "beautiful garden", you can
expect a "lovely meal" – and a "pricey" check.

Home Port *New England/Seafood*

20 **17** **18** **$47**

Menemsha | 512 North Rd. (Basin Rd.) | 508-645-2679 |
www.homeportmv.com

"Thank God" this nearly 80-year-old BYO seafood "legend" in
Menemsha "has been spared" from closing and the new owners who
bought it in early 2009 plan to keep it "chugging along" with the same
"simply prepared", "fresh seafood" (it costs "a lot of money", "but at
least the portions are large"); there's a "cramped, loud" dining room,
but there's also "fabulous takeout" to "eat on picnic tables" or, better
still, bring to the beach for a "beautiful sunset" meal.

Jimmy Seas Pan Pasta *Italian*

23 **13** **19** **$34**

Oak Bluffs | 38 Kennebec Ave. (off Post Office Sq.) | 508-696-8550

"They roast garlic like nobody's business" at this Oak Bluffs Italian, so
"follow your nose" and "bring a hearty appetite" for "hot, steamy
pans" of "fantastic pasta" and "fabulous seafood" served in portions
"mammoth" "enough to feed a small army" (expect a surcharge if you
"plan to split"); just "get there early" or be prepared for an "awful
wait" to be "scrunched" into the "tiny", "noisy" space.

Lambert's Cove Inn *American*

25 **26** **25** **$60**

West Tisbury | Lambert's Cove Inn & Restaurant | 90 Manaquayak Rd.
(Lambert's Cove Rd.) | 508-693-2298 | www.lambertscoveinn.com

Check into this "lovely", "British-y" dining room in a "charming country inn" "nestled" in West Tisbury, a "romantic" place where "you can
have a private conversation" while savoring views of a "slice-of-
heaven" garden and "superb" American cuisine made with "excellent

FOOD | DECOR | SERVICE | COST

ingredients" and "presented in delicate, unique ways"; "impeccable" servers add to the "terrific evening", which is expectedly "expensive", even though you have to "bring your own alcohol."

Larsen's Fish Market *Seafood*

27 | 10 | 20 | $23

Menemsha | 56 Basin Rd. (North Rd.) | 508-645-2680

"Basically a take-out place within a fish market", this Menemsha counter doles out "cardboard plates of oysters, shucked in front of your eyes", "luscious lobster rolls", "freshly steamed steamers" and other "amazingly fresh", "simple" seafood "right off the boat"; it's "all to be eaten outside" on "wooden crates" or at "the beach watching the sunset" – an "unforgettable meal", and a "reasonable" one at that.

Lattanzi's *Italian*

21 | 17 | 20 | $48

Edgartown | Old Post Office Sq. (bet. Main & Winter Sts.) | 508-627-8854 | www.lattanzis.com

Go for the "cozy, elegant" "fine-dining option" or the casual "pizza division" with a "nice patio" at this "delightful" Edgartown *duetto* where "innovative" Tuscan touches abound in "great" thin-crust, brick-oven pies, pastas and other "Italian comfort foods", all "solid values"; whichever side you choose, the "friendly" staff "cares to have you as a guest."

Le Grenier *French*

23 | 16 | 23 | $51

Vineyard Haven | 92 Main St. (bet. Church St. & Colonial Ln.) | 508-693-4906 | www.legrenierrestaurant.com

"As old as the money that makes it successful", this Vineyard Haven BYO with an "awkward" location "up a long flight of stairs" and a rustic setting with exposed beams "perfectly executes" "classical French cuisine", which is brought to table by "delightful" staffers; the "stagnant menu" "may run against the tide of modernity", but the "core group of stalwarts" that frequents it declares "it's nice to have the choice available."

L'Étoile *French*

26 | 26 | 23 | $73

Edgartown | 22 N. Water St. (Winter St.) | 508-627-5187 | www.letoile.net

"Save up for a special occasion" (like "popping the question"), then make a reservation for this New French "delight" in Edgartown delivering "wonderful everything": "exceptional" cuisine, wines and surroundings, which include a "relaxing bar" with a "lighter menu"; in addition, already "efficient" servers "go the extra mile for you", ensuring a wholly "lovely evening."

Lola's ● Cajun/Creole

22 | 22 | 20 | $41

Oak Bluffs | 15 Island Inn Rd. (Beach Rd.) | 508-693-5007 |
www.lolassouthernseafood.com

"Nothing else comes close to what you find" at this "spirited, inviting"
Oak Bluffs venue where "large groups of families and friends" come
for "fantastic", "reasonably priced" Cajun-Creole dishes, "many with
fresh local seafood", served alongside "exciting live music"; later in
the evening, "younger" folks "party on" with "dancing and drinks"
brought by staffers that stay "enthusiastic" while "clearly over-
extended"; P.S. the "hearty" Sunday jazz brunch is also "fabulous."

Lure American

▽ 21 | 21 | 22 | $68

Edgartown | Winnetu Oceanside Resort | 31 Dunes Rd. (Katama Rd.) |
508-627-3663 | www.luremv.com

"If weather permits", take the "delightful" complimentary water taxi
from Edgartown to this "cavernous" New American at the Winnetu
Oceanside Resort for a "grown-up" New American meal in the "civi-
ized dining room" or on the patio; "if you can't find a sitter", you'll be
relegated to a separate space, the milieu of toys and "chicken fingers"
but "pleasant" nonetheless – just come "before dark", because it's
"priced more for the scenery than for the food."

Net Result Seafood

25 | 12 | 19 | $21

Vineyard Haven | Tisbury Marketplace | 79 Beach Rd. (Lagoon Pond Rd.) |
508-693-6071 | www.mvseafood.com

"For a true taste of the sea", join the line for this "often-crowded"
"dockside seafood store with a carry-out kitchen" in Vineyard Haven,
where "incredibly fresh" fish and "wonderfully prepared sushi" are
"cheerfully provided" "at affordable prices"; there are "a few picnic tables available" outside, but they fill up quickly, so you're probably better off heading to the "nearby beach."

Newes from America Pub Food

18 | 20 | 19 | $28

Edgartown | Kelley House | 23 Kelley St. (N. Water St.) | 508-627-4397 |
www.kelley-house.com

It "feels like a whaling-ship captain may walk in at any moment" to this
"cozy", "welcoming" "Colonial-era building" that's "everything a New
England pub should be": a "laid-back" haunt for "generous servings" of
"quality", "reasonably priced" sandwiches, burgers and snacks to soak

	FOOD	DECOR	SERVICE	COST

up "excellent beers"; no wonder "locals congregate here year-round" to "catch a ballgame" on TV while chatting with the "nice folks" on staff.

Offshore Ale Co. *American* | 20 | 20 | 19 | $27 |

Oak Bluffs | 30 Kennebec Ave. (Healey Way) | 508-693-2626 | www.offshoreale.com

"Kids of all ages love the free baskets of peanuts (or perhaps they just love throwing the shells on the floor)" at this Oak Bluffs brewpub, but there's more to adore than that, namely "nonpretentious" American grub ("phenomenal pizzas", "great burgers", etc.) and "incredible homemade beers", all "affordable"; the "occasional live band" keeps it "absolutely fun", even in winter when there's a "fire going."

☑ Outermost Inn Ⓜ *American* | 25 | 26 | 23 | $85 |

Aquinnah | Outermost Inn | 81 Lighthouse Rd. (State Rd.) | 508-645-3511 | www.outermostinn.com

For the ultimate "romantic getaway", "leave the kids with a sitter" (they're not allowed if they're under 12) and head to this "spectacular" New American in a "lovely" ocean-view Aquinnah inn for an "imaginative, well-prepared" and "extremely pricey" prix fixe; a "terrific" staff buoys the "elegant but casual" vibe, which is even more of a "special treat" if you get to "see the sunset"; P.S. the BYO policy "has gone by the wayside."

Park Corner Bistro *American* | ▽ 22 | 20 | 20 | $47 |

Oak Bluffs | 20H Kennebec Ave. (off Circuit Ave.) | 508-696-9922 | www.parkcornerbistro.com

While it's "on a busy corner in Oak Bluffs", this "tiny" spot with an equally "intimate bar" "never feels rushed or noisy" while its "sweet and attentive" staff ferries "interesting" American bistro fare with French influences and "great cocktails"; after some recent changes in focus, tough customers feel it still "has to decide what it is", but even they can't resist the "terrific brunch."

🆕 Salt Water Ⓢ *Eclectic* | - | - | - | M |

Vineyard Haven | Tisbury Marketplace | 79 Beach Rd. (off Beach St. & Water St.) | 508-338-4666 | www.saltwaterrestaurant.com

Early admirers call this Eclectic BYO a "great addition to Vineyard Haven", especially since there's plenty of room in the "sparse", "pleasant" dining room (with vaulted ceilings, many windows and sweeping view of a lagoon) to sample its "enjoyable" all-day wares; there are a few reports of sketchy service, but "maybe it needs time" to find its sea legs.

Sharky's Cantina ● *Mexican*

21 | **20** | **20** | **$20**

NEW **Edgartown** | 266 Upper Main St. (Chase Rd.) | 508-627-6565
Oak Bluffs | 31 Circuit Ave. (Narragansett Ave.) | 508-693-7501 |
www.sharkyscantina.com

"Don't expect miracles" and you'll have "fun" at these "kitschy" Edgartown and Oak Bluffs Mexican "joints" that are always "loaded with locals and tourists" digging into "big stuffed burritos" and other "standard fare"; "reasonable prices" make it an option "for the whole family", while a heady selection of tequilas and "great margaritas" abet "special times out for grown-ups."

NEW Sidecar Café & Bar *New England*

– | – | – | I

Oak Bluffs | 16 Kennebec Ave. (Lake Ave.) | 508-693-6261 |
www.sidecarcafeandbar.com

At this Oak Bluffs newcomer, the New England fare exhibits some "memorable" Italian flair and "beautiful execution" that "speaks of a chef and owner who care about what they are doing", even as they keep prices low; the light, intimate space displays local art, the bar is a "great" place to "meet for drinks" and the sidewalk tables prove to be an entertaining vantage point for "people-watching."

Slice of Life *American*

– | – | – | M

Oak Bluffs | 50 Circuit Ave. (bet. Lake & Samoset Aves.) | 508-693-3838 |
www.sliceoflifemv.com

This quaint, all-day, year-round cafe just a stone's throw from the ocean in Oak Bluffs may not have water views or outdoor seating, but it has cultivated a loyal following that starts its day at the espresso bar with a pastry, picks up a specialty sandwich for lunch and then returns for moderately priced New American dinners; a post-Survey change of ownership was expected, but not any changes.

Sweet Life Café *American*

25 | **22** | **23** | **$62**

Oak Bluffs | 63 Circuit Ave. (bet. Narragansett & Pequot Aves.) |
508-696-0200 | www.sweetlifemv.com

Lovers of this "jewel of a find in Oak Bluffs" keep "searching for an excuse" to go back for its "just wonderful" New American–New French "gourmet home cooking"; the restored Victorian setting is "beautiful indoors or out" ("if you can, eat in the garden") and an especially "lovely spot for date night", made even more attractive by "friendly, attentive" staffers (if not the "prices you're paying").

Theo's *American*

▽ 24 | 25 | 24 | $50

Chilmark | Inn at Blueberry Hill | 74 North Rd. (bet. Old Farm Rd. & Tea Ln.) | 508-645-3322 | www.blueberryinn.com

Set on "beautiful" former farmlands in Chilmark, this New American maintains a "perfectly nice, long" "enclosed porch" on which to serve "consistently good" fare (pricey, but the "Sunday rustic suppers are a bargain"); besides the "heavenly" setting, "wonderfully relaxed" meals are achieved via staffers who are "so focused" on their customers, who in turn breathe easy having remembered to bring their own alcohol.

NEW Waterside Market *American*

- | - | - | M

Vineyard Haven | 76 Main St. (Union St.) | 508-693-8899 | www.watersidemarket.com

Not far from the ferry terminal in Vineyard Haven, this homey, moderately priced newcomer is a cafe, coffee bar, specialty-foods market and generally "easy stop" for a "wide selection" of American breakfasts and lunches made with "fresh ingredients" by an "enthusiastic staff."

NEW Water St. *Eclectic*

- | - | - | E

Edgartown | Harbor View Hotel & Resort | 131 N. Water St. (Cottage St.) | 508-627-7000 | www.harbor-view.com

Newly opened and already "living up to" its "spectacular" setting in the Harborview Hotel & Resort, this "beautiful room" pairs panoramas of Edgartown Harbor with "delightful", "creative" Eclectic cuisine utilizing seasonal ingredients and "cooked to perfection"; "excellent" service is another aspect that elicits a sincere "wow."

Zapotec *Southwestern*

19 | 16 | 21 | $29

Oak Bluffs | 14 Kennebec Ave. (Lake Ave.) | 508-693-6800 | www.zapotecrestaurant.com

Southwestern fare may seem "incongruous on the Vineyard", however, it is what's for dinner at this "old" Oak Bluffs "cottage"; the tabs are "inexpensive", but "you have to put up with" bright, "cheesy decorations" and a "small, overcrowded space" to get them; "be prepared to wait" when its "busy", perhaps at the bar, since the fare's "better" after "a pretty good margarita" or two.

Zephrus *American*

| 20 | 19 | 20 | $38 |

Vineyard Haven | Mansion House | 9 Main St. (State Rd.) | 508-693-3416 | www.zephrus.com

This Vineyard Haven hotel BYO blows hot and cold – the "enjoyable" "screened-in porch" trumps the "uninspired" interior, and the New American fare is "somewhat uneven" (the "standards" are "solid", while the "innovations" "could use some attention"), just as the menu "varies wildly in price" (thankfully, it's mostly "reasonable"); one fact, however, is indisputable: the "convenient location" is "hard to beat."

Nantucket

Alice's Restaurant *American/Thai*

| ▽ 18 | 12 | 18 | $30 |

Nantucket | Nantucket Airport | 14 Airport Rd. (Old South Rd.) | 508-228-6005

Fans aver the all-day American-Thai fare at this "dependable", moderately priced Nantucket airport eatery is "worth flying in for" – critics of "strange menus", on the other hand, would order "only if stranded"; one thing's for sure, "you can't beat the view if you like planes."

American Seasons *American*

| 25 | 23 | 22 | $67 |

Nantucket | 80 Centre St. (W. Chester St.) | 508-228-7111 | www.americanseasons.com

"Each visit is a voyage of discovery" at this folksy, "candlelit" Nantucket "foodies' paradise" where "genius" chef/co-owner Michael LaScola turns "cutting-edge ingredients" into "knock-your-socks-off" New American regional riffs listed under the headings Down South, New England and Pacific Coast; some object to "spending lots" for sometimes "haughty" (though "knowledgeable") service, but they're drowned out by groupies clinking glasses of "stellar all-American wines."

Arno's *American*

| 16 | 15 | 16 | $36 |

Nantucket | 41 Main St. (bet. Federal & Orange Sts.) | 508-228-7001 | www.arnos.net

"Breakfast is the best bet" at this "cozy" bi-level "Nantucket original", while, "depending on the day", the American comfort-food lunches and dinners swing between "so-so" and "great"; nevertheless, it's an "old standby" for families since it's "reasonably priced" ("hard to find" on Nantucket).

Black-Eyed Susan's ⊯ *American* | 26 | 15 | 21 | $36 |

Nantucket | 10 India St. (Centre St.) | 508-325-0308 |
www.black-eyedsusans.com

"Everyone raves" about the "fantastic" American breakfasts at this "funky", "dinerlike" "Nantucket classic", but "dinners are also amazing"; even though BYO "keeps prices down", the cash-only policy is an "unpleasant surprise" for some – as are the "ridiculously long waits" and often "loud, hot" digs; escaping the "cramped" tables by "sitting at the counter and watching the short-order show", meanwhile, often generates happy revelations.

Boarding House *American* | 21 | 19 | 20 | $62 |

Nantucket | 12 Federal St. (India St.) | 508-228-9622 |
www.boardinghouse-pearl.com

"Earthy", "inventive" New American fare made with "quality" market-driven ingredients ("expensive relative to off-island" but "not the highest on Nantucket") is what's for dinner at this more "humble" sibling to "flashy" Pearl next door; most opt for the "unparalleled social scene" and "great people-watching" on the patio ("worth the wait" for), but there are also admirers of the "crowded, noisy" bar and "romantically lit" cellar, even though it's "still a basement."

Brant Point Grill *American* | 21 | 24 | 21 | $64 |

Nantucket | White Elephant Hotel | 50 Easton St. (Harbor View Way) | 508-228-2500 | www.whiteelephanthotel.com

"Killer views" of Nantucket Harbor and "convenience" draw guests of the White Elephant Hotel to its all-day eatery for "well-prepared" New American dishes and drinks at the "friendly bar"; locals, on the other hand, peg it as "just a tiny bit boring" for being so "pricey."

Brotherhood of Thieves *American* | 18 | 20 | 18 | $33 |

Nantucket | 23 Broad St. (bet. Centre & Federal Sts.) | 508-228-2551 |
www.brotherhoodofthieves.com

Dispelling the notion that "everyone on Nantucket wears Ralph Lauren", this "unpretentious" "tradition" gives "families" "bang for the buck" with "hearty" pub-leaning American grub ("don't leave without sampling the curly fries" and "awesome burgers"); the "modern" upstairs "isn't as cozy" as the "rustic" brick-and-beam "watering-hole"-like space downstairs, but the "best seats in the house" may in fact be outside.

FOOD | DECOR | SERVICE | COST

Cambridge Street ☒Ⓜ *Eclectic*

| - | - | - | M |

Nantucket | 12 Cambridge St. (New South Rd.) | 508-228-7109

The local artwork on the walls and "young people" at the bar are "worth watching" at this "funky little bistro", just as the "fun", "inventive" Eclectic eats – starring "great burgers", thin-crust pizzas and barbecue – merit noshing; despite the hip scene up front, a children's menu and "reasonable prices" mean it's family-friendly at the tables.

Centre Street Bistro *American*

| ▽ 16 | 11 | 12 | $34 |

Nantucket | Meeting House | 29 Centre St. (bet. Chestnut & India Sts.) | 508-228-8470 | www.nantucketbistro.com

If you're a Nantucket local, you'll end up at this New American Meeting House eatery with "limited atmosphere" in the off-season because, even though it's a crapshoot whether you'll "leave hungry" or "satisfied", it's "cheap"; likewise, if you're a summer tourist, you'll be "caught" here "when you run out of money – and you will."

Chanticleer Ⓜ *French*

| 25 | 25 | 24 | $76 |

Siasconset | 9 New St. (Milestone Rd.) | 508-257-6231 | www.thechanticleer.net

There are "no rivals in Siasconset" fawn fans of this "Nantucket classic" where "languorous lunches" and "romantic dinners" star "excellent wines" and "spectacular" French cuisine created with "local seafood and produce"; dining outside "beneath a canopy of roses" and among "beautiful hydrangeas" is "lovely", while the "elegant" interior rooms "do justice to the historic" cottage – but all that's not enough to impress numbers-crunchers who calculate it's "not worth the exalted prices."

Cinco *Nuevo Latino*

| ▽ 26 | 24 | 25 | $69 |

Nantucket | 5 Amelia Dr. (Old South Rd.) | 508-325-5151 | www.cinco5.com

"Islanders would rather you didn't know about" this "comfortable" Nantucket "gem" where "enthusiastic", "helpful servers guide" you in choosing from the "intriguing" variety of "creative" Nuevo Latino tapas and "super" Spanish wines; the "romantic", "candlelit", modern-art-bedecked spot is "a touch out of the way", which means they can keep "dancing on the patio" among themselves – at least for the time being.

Cioppino's *American*
19 | 17 | 20 | $47

Nantucket | 20 Broad St. (bet. Centre & Federal Sts.) | 508-228-4622 | www.cioppinos.com
"You won't go wrong" if you order the namesake seafood-and-pasta dish at this "stalwart" in an old, cozy clapboard home, and although some culinary critics judge it "doesn't always get" all of its New American cuisine "right", the "great variety" and "large portions" equal "values"; the "charismatic" staff adds to a vibe that's "friendly in all respects", and relaxing too, especially on the "excellent patio."

Club Car *Continental*
20 | 19 | 21 | $64

Nantucket | 1 Main St. (Easy St.) | 508-228-1101 | www.theclubcar.com
Traditionalists get "old-style" Continental "classics" from "fabulous" staffers at this "simple, white-tablecloth" "charmer" "in the heart of town", and afterwards, they join other "rich weekenders and singles over 40" in the "crowded, fun bar" – a "high-style" annex set in a 19th-century railway club car – for "live piano" and "creative drinks"; only modernists can't jump onboard, dissing "so-so", "sauce-on-every-thing" preparations and "inflated prices."

❷ Company of the Cauldron *American*
28 | 24 | 25 | $71

Nantucket | 5 India St. (bet. Centre & Federal Sts.) | 508-228-4016 | www.companyofthecauldron.com
"Ethereal" meals are conjured nightly at this "cozy", "friendly" "romantic" offering an "ever-changing, ever-inspired" New American prix fixe in "a dinner-party-like environment" with harp music (three nights a week) and candlelight; the set menu can be a "deal breaker for picky eaters" (especially considering it's so costly), but for "true gourmands", it's the "most innovative and rewarding experience" Nantucket has to offer.

DeMarco *Italian*
22 | 18 | 20 | $67

Nantucket | 9 India St. (bet. Centre & Federal Sts.) | 508-228-1836 | www.demarcorestaurant.com
"Thirty years in the same location" and it's "still got it" applaud acolytes of this venture proffering an "upscale" Northern Italian menu ("somewhat limited" but often "amazing") in a "charming" 19th-century townhouse; it's often packed, so "if you can't get a table" in the "bit-cramped upstairs" dining room, ask the "welcoming, attentive" staff to find you a spot at the "lively, attractive bar."

	FOOD	DECOR	SERVICE	COST

Even Keel Cafe *American*

| 19 | 14 | 16 | $31 |

Nantucket | 40 Main St. (Federal St.) | 508-228-1979 |
www.evenkeelcafe.com

From sunup to well after sundown, it's "smooth sailing" at this "unas-
suming little place" with a "beautiful, serene" patio – at least as far as
the "bountiful", "reliable", "reasonably priced" New American fare is
concerned; when it comes to service, well, when it's "busy", "you
might keel over before you even get" a "cup of coffee."

Fifty-Six Union *Eclectic*

| 22 | 21 | 23 | $63 |

Nantucket | 56 Union St. (E. Dover St.) | 508-228-6135 |
www.fiftysixunion.com

"Nobody's worried about who's who" at this "year-round gem" "on
the edge of town" – what draws "mingling natives" is the "attentive
service" and "creative" Eclectic fare ("not an expansive menu,
but each item is choice"); yes, this is "serious food", but "you can
take the kids", especially if you choose the more "bistro"-like of
the two interior rooms (bedecked with local art and sculptures)
or the patio.

Fog Island Cafe *American*

| 21 | 15 | 19 | $21 |

Nantucket | 7 S. Water St. (India St.) | 508-228-1818 |
www.fogisland.com

Not only is this "cozy", basic cafe a "great spot" for "delicious, hearty,
healthy", "quick breakfasts" ("especially for families", because it's
cheap), but it also "gets the juices flowing" with New American
lunches and in-season dinners; "weather permitting", ask the
"friendly", "attentive" servers to find you a spot "out back" to "enjoy
the ocean air."

☑ Galley Beach *Eclectic*

| 24 | 27 | 23 | $78 |

Nantucket | 54 Jefferson Ave. (off N. Beach St.) | 508-228-9641

If "spectacular sunsets", a "beautiful beach" setting with "waves
crashing in the background" and "fantastic food" are "what you pine
for", book this "famously romantic" sand-side spot whose "phenomenal" outdoor "real estate" and "out-of-this-world" Eclectic cuisine are
"worth" "paying through the nose for"; also on deck is a "professional
staff" trained to anticipate "every need" of its patrons, on whom "blue
blazers, stripes and khakis" abound.

	FOOD	DECOR	SERVICE	COST

Jetties, The *Italian/New England* ▽ 14 | 18 | 11 | $25

Nantucket | 4 Bathing Beach Rd. (Hulbert Ave.) | 508-228-2279 |
www.thejettiesnantucket.com

"For family fun, you can't beat" this "very casual" Italian-New Englander,
as the "kids can play on the beach while you have an adult conversation"
on the deck or a drink while listening to the occasional "nice live music" at the bar; just make sure you're well into vacation mode, because
the "lackluster food" is "lackadaisically served" (it's cheap at least).

Le Languedoc Bistro *French* 26 | 22 | 25 | $63

Nantucket | Le Languedoc Inn | 24 Broad St. (bet. Centre & Federal Sts.) |
508-228-2552 | www.lelanguedoc.com

"All the classics" plus "enough inventiveness to keep you coming
back" "year after year" – not to mention "an appealing wine list" – is
the "tantalizing" formula at this "lovely" French "gem" with a patio, a
more formal dining room and a "cozy" bistro/bar below ("cheaper
than upstairs" but still "*très* delicious"); the staff's simultaneous "professional" and "laid-back" tone adds to an experience enthusiasts
cheer is "wonderful in every way."

Lo La 41° ◑ *Eclectic* 21 | 22 | 20 | $55

Nantucket | 15 S. Beach St. (Sea St.) | 508-325-4001 | www.lola41.net

"High-octane" to the nth degree, this "chicly decorated", "intimate
spot" is known more for a "wildly hopping" "bar scene", but its "black
Armani"-sporting habitués say the Eclectic victuals (there's a "great
sushi" menu as well as a bistro *carte*) are "fantastic" too; however,
holdouts warn the "small portions" are "way too expensive, even for
Nantucket", and the "noise level is impossible" (next time, they might
try the "divine patio").

Nantucket Lobster Trap *Seafood* 19 | 15 | 18 | $46

Nantucket | 23 Washington St. (Coffin St.) | 508-228-4200 |
www.nantucketlobstertrap.com

"If you've got a hankering for no-frills lobster", this "institution of
shirt-staining" is "the place to go" for "more than ample portions" of
"decent seafood" at "low prices" ("for the island"); the servers do
their best to be "nice and accommodating" while getting "high vol-
umes" of "tourists" fed and out of the "bland", "noisy" environs, but
there's "always a line" of more waiting to get in.

	FOOD	DECOR	SERVICE	COST

Òran Mór *Eclectic*
24 | 23 | 24 | $75

Nantucket | 2 S. Beach St. (Whalers Ln.) | 508-228-8655 |
www.oranmorbistro.com

An "awe-inspiring" "use of seasonal ingredients" is the forte of this "enchanting" Eclectic, as "unforgettable" for its "remarkable" fare as it is for an "elegant", "quaint" setting up a flight of "copper stairs" ("perfect for a romantic rendezvous"); in accord with the "veritable symphony" of tastes are an "excellent wine list" and an "attentive staff", and while it's "not cheap", "if anyplace on this expensive island is worth it", it's this one.

Pearl *Asian Fusion/French*
24 | 25 | 22 | $69

Nantucket | 12 Federal St. (India St.) | 508-228-9701 |
www.boardinghouse-pearl.com

"Hip" folks who "want it all" find it at this Asian fusion–New French "party" that entices with a "tremendous bar", "delicious libations", "friendly, helpful servers" and "cool", "unexpected decor" that reminds them of weekends spent in "New York"/"LA"/"Miami"/"Monte Carlo"; the "innovative" fare is "fabulous" too, although belt-tighteners blanch "it's hard to enjoy the fresh fish when you're gagging on the prices."

Pi Pizzeria *Pizza*
∇ 23 | 12 | 20 | $32

Nantucket | 11 W. Creek Rd. (bet. Orange & Pleasant Sts.) | 508-228-1130 |
www.pipizzeria.com

"Escape the buzz of Downtown" Nantucket and get "your pizza fix" all in one fell swoop at this parlor baking wood-fired, thin-crust Neapolitan "lusciousness" and additional moderately priced Italian dishes of "solid quality"; there's "always a line" for a table, but takeout is an option, as is the bar.

Queequeg's *Eclectic*
25 | 20 | 24 | $48

Nantucket | 6 Oak St. (Fedral St.) | 508-325-0992 |
www.queequegsnantucket.com

"What a treat!" cheer boosters of this "casual" "little jewel" "in the heart of N'tucket town", where the "nice variety" of Eclectic eats is "delightful and delicious all-around", not to mention "reasonably priced" (in island terms); bonus points are earned because "you can usually get a table" in the "snug", "lovely", whale-art-sporting interior, if not on the "adorable" deck.

Ropewalk, The *Seafood*

| - | - | - | M |

Nantucket | 1 Straight Wharf (Easy St.) | 508-228-8886 |
www.theropewalk.com

Taking its name from its past as a building where ropes for ships were
made, this waterside seafooder boasts an outdoor patio, three dining
rooms, two drinks bars, a raw bar and breathtaking views of Nantucket
Harbor; it's quite a hip scene, but moderate prices make it smart
for families too.

Sconset Café ⊄ *American*

| 21 | 16 | 19 | $48 |

Siasconset | 8 Main St. (Post Office Sq.) | 508-257-4008 |
www.sconsetcafe.com

"Run by 'Sconseters for 'Sconseters", this "charming", "cash-only"
New American provides "homemade muffins" for breakfast, "great
sandwiches after a bike ride" in the afternoon and "fresh, lively" dinners amid candlelight and "ever-changing exhibits of local artists";
service can be "slow" when "crowded", but you're on "island time", so
just "relax" and pour another glass from the stash you picked up at the
wine-and-books store next door.

SeaGrille *Seafood*

| 22 | 17 | 21 | $49 |

Nantucket | 45 Sparks Ave. (bet. Pleasant St. & Sanford Rd.) | 508-325-5700 |
www.theseagrille.com

Sure, this "Nantucket tradition" "provides the seafood staples", but it
"can also cut loose" with "marvelous" "daily specials"; the digs may be
slightly "dated", but as long as it continues to remain "open year-
round", "make everyone feel welcome" (especially "families" with
"kids") and deliver "value", "locals" will keep on recommending it as
a "solid performer."

Sfoglia ⊠ *Italian*

| 24 | 18 | 21 | $62 |

Nantucket | 130 Pleasant St. (bet. Chins Way & W. Creek Rd.) |
508-325-4500 | www.sfogliarestaurant.com

"High-quality fresh ingredients" are evident in the "creative" fare proffered at this Italian, which employs "friendly, attentive" staffers to
"help guide" diners through the "limited, quirky menu" ("pricey", but
"worth it for the bread" alone); both private and "communal tables" fill
the "just-redesigned", "shabby-chic" setting, which some aesthetes
"don't really dig."

	FOOD	DECOR	SERVICE	COST

Ships Inn *Californian/French*

	24	22	22	$68

Nantucket | Ships Inn | 13 Fair St. (Lucretia Mott Ln.) | 508-228-0040 |
www.shipsinnnantucket.com

Only "knowledgeable Nantucketers dine" at this "seasonal" "gem" serving "superb", "creative" Californian-French fare, since it's virtually "hidden" in the "basement" of an 18th-century whaling captain's mansion; it's "on the edge of town", so couples can take "a romantic walk" at the end of their "lovely evening" – but the "friendly staff" and "inviting", "cozy bar" make many "want to linger."

Slip 14 *American*

	18	17	19	$48

Nantucket | 14 Old South Wharf (New Whale St.) | 508-228-2033 |
www.slip14.com

"Finish up your Nantucket jaunt" at this "casual" New American "family" "respite" near the ferries, which offers "wonderful outdoor seating" on a "fun wharf" (inside's a little "dark"); dollar-watchers who deem the vittles "overpriced" for being only "ok" stick to "sweet specialty cocktails" at the bar, which hops with a "twentysomething crowd in the evening."

Straight Wharf *Seafood*

	25	25	24	$73

Nantucket | 6 Harbor Sq. (Straight Wharf) | 508-228-4499 |
www.straightwharfrestaurant.com

"On a summer night", there may not be a more "gorgeous" or "romantic" setting than the dining porch "overlooking the harbor" at this "standout", but the "absolutely beautiful" interior is an equally "tantalizing" "Nantucket habitat" in which to enjoy "inspiring" "high-end seafood" that "utilizes local ingredients effectively"; a "split personality" emerges later in the evening when "jocks" and their quarry create a "lively bar scene", which is "thankfully, separated from the main room."

Summer House *American*

	20	23	19	$71

Siasconset | Summer House | 17 Ocean Ave. (Magnolia Ave.) |
508-257-9976 | www.thesummerhouse.com

A "pianist plays delightful music to accompany" New American meals in this "very expensive" Siasconset inn's "simple but elegant" main room (off of which sits a "great old porch"), while ocean breezes cool at its "beachside bistro"; yes, its location on the coast is undeniably "beautiful", but with "hit-or-miss" dishes and occasional "attitude" from the staff, some suspect it "coasts on the location."

Sushi by Yoshi *Japanese* | 25 | 13 | 19 | $37 |

Nantucket | 2 E. Chestnut St. (Water St.) | 508-228-1801 |
www.sushibyyoshi.com

Nantucketers feel "lucky to have a sushi place" that's as "inventive",
"super-fresh" and "affordable" as this "jewel"; some say it's "worth
the wait" to eat in the "small" "mob scene" ("BYOB, baby!"), but many
feel it's "better to do takeout" – the rolls and sashimi "travel well."

☑ Topper's *American* | 27 | 27 | 26 | $95 |

Nantucket | Wauwinet Inn | 120 Wauwinet Rd. (2 mi. north of Polpis Rd.) |
508-228-8768 | www.wauwinet.com

"Stuff your wallet" with "big bucks", take the "romantic" "water shuttle"
"across the harbor from town" and get to this "special-occasion spot" at
the Wauwinet Inn "in time to see the sunset"; next up is the "divine culinary experience" of chef David Daniels' "handsomely plated", "exquisite" New American cuisine, which is presented by "impeccable" servers
alongside a "deftly crafted wine list" in a "beautiful" dining room and
"lovely", less-formal patio – just "don't expect large portions" and "you
won't be disappointed"; P.S. lunch and brunch are just as "memorable."

29 Fair Street Ⓜ *Continental* | 22 | 23 | 19 | $63 |

Nantucket | 29 Fair St. (Martins Ln.) | 508-228-7800 | www.29fair.com
The owners of the "famed Summer House" have turned the old
Woodbox restaurant, set in a 300-year-old building, into this
Continental "hideaway" where diners "venture back in time" via three
candlelit rooms sporting original brick fireplaces, exposed beams and
antique sconces; boosters find the pricey offerings "great", while a minority pronounces them merely fair, citing a "limited menu" filled with
dishes that are "not unique" enough.

☑ 21 Federal *American* | 24 | 23 | 23 | $68 |

Nantucket | 21 Federal St. (bet. Chestnut & Oak Sts.) | 508-228-2121 |
www.21federal.com

"After all these years", this "quintessential" Nantucket New American
in a "handsome", "romantic" Greek Revival edifice complete with a
"charming patio" still "pampers" via "delectable creations" made with
"local provender" that virtually "dances on the plate"; though a few
critics carp that it's "way too expensive" (and perhaps "pretentious"),
Federalists affirm it "should never change."

Cuisines

Includes restaurant names, locations and Food ratings.

AMERICAN (NEW)

Alchemy	MV	22
Alice's	Nan	18
American Seasons	Nan	25
Aqua Grille	CC	19
Atria	MV	25
Balance	MV	23
Barley Neck Inn	CC	20
Bayside Betsy's	CC	15
Beach Plum	MV	25
Belfry Inne	CC	25
Bistro/Crowne Pointe	CC	22
Black-Eyed Susan's	Nan	26
NEW Blackfish	CC	24
Boarding Hse.	Nan	21
☑ Bramble Inn	CC	27
Brant Point	Nan	21
Cafe Edwige/at Night	CC	26
Cape Sea Grille	CC	26
Centre St. Bistro	Nan	16
Chapoquoit Grill	CC	22
Chatham Bars Inn	CC	22
Cioppino's	Nan	19
Circadia Bistro	CC	23
☑ Company/Cauldron	Nan	28
Dan'l Webster	CC	20
☑ Détente	MV	27
Devon's	CC	24
Even Keel	Nan	19
Finely JP's	CC	21
Fishmonger's	CC	18
Five Bays Bistro	CC	25
Fog Island	Nan	21
Heather	CC	-
Island Merchant	CC	-
Lure	MV	21
Mews	CC	27

Ocean House	CC	25
☑ Outermost Inn	MV	25
Park Corner	MV	22
Port	CC	23
☑ Red Pheasant	CC	27
Regatta of Cotuit	CC	25
RooBar	CC	21
Ross' Grill	CC	22
Scargo Café	CC	20
Sconset Café	Nan.	21
Sweet/Slice Life	MV	-
Slip 14	Nan	18
Summer House	Nan.	20
Sweet/Slice Life	MV	25
Terra Luna	CC	24
Theo's	MV	24
☑ Topper's	Nan	27
☑ 28 Atlantic	CC	26
☑ 21 Federal	Nan	24
Wicked Oyster	CC	24
Winslow's Tavern	CC	20
Zephrus	MV	20

AMERICAN (TRADITIONAL)

Adrian's	CC	16
Art Cliff Diner	MV	24
Bee-Hive Tavern	CC	19
Betsy's Diner	CC	18
☑ Black Dog Tavern	MV	19
Brotherhood/Thieves	Nan	18
Capt. Kidd	CC	18
Capt. Linnell	CC	22
Capt. Parker's	CC	18
Cioppino's	Nan	19
Clancy's	CC	22
Coonamessett Inn	CC	18

David Ryan's | **MV** 15
Dolphin | **CC** 21
Fairway | **CC** 18
Fanizzi's | **CC** 20
Lambert's Cove | **MV** 25
Laura & Tony's | **CC** -
Marshside | **CC** 15
Newes/America | **MV** 18
☑ Not Average Joe's | **CC** 18
Offshore Ale | **MV** 20
Optimist Café | **CC** 21
Orleans Inn | **CC** 17
Post Office | **CC** 16
NEW Waterside Mkt. | **MV** -
Whitman House | **CC** 21
Wild Goose | **CC** 21

ASIAN FUSION

HannaH's Fusion | **CC** 24
Pearl | **Nan** 24

BRAZILIAN

Brazilian Grill | **CC** 21

BRITISH

Dunbar Tea | **CC** 22
Optimist Café | **CC** 21

BURGERS

Brotherhood/Thieves | **Nan** 18

CAJUN

Lola's | **MV** 22

CALIFORNIAN

Ships Inn | **Nan** 24

CAMBODIAN

Stir Crazy | **CC** 23

CARIBBEAN

Island Merchant | **CC** -

COFFEE SHOPS/ DINERS

Art Cliff Diner | **MV** 24
Betsy's Diner | **CC** 18

CONTINENTAL

Anthony Cummaquid | **CC** 18
Club Car | **Nan** 20
☑ Front St. | **CC** 27
29 Fair St. | **Nan** 22

CREOLE

Lola's | **MV** 22

ECLECTIC

Academy Ocean | **CC** 22
Bubala's | **CC** 16
Cambridge St. | **Nan** -
Chatham Squire | **CC** 18
Chesca's | **MV** 23
Fifty-Six Union | **Nan** 22
Firefly Woodfire | **CC** 20
☑ Galley Beach | **Nan** 24
Laureen's | **CC** 23
Lobster Pot | **CC** 22
Lo La 41° | **Nan** 21
Napi's | **CC** 19
Òran Mór | **Nan** 24
Queequeg's | **Nan** 25
NEW Salt Water | **MV** -
Vining's Bistro | **CC** 24
NEW Water St. | **MV** -

FRENCH

Bleu | **CC** 25
Chanticleer | **Nan.** 25
☑ Chillingsworth | **CC** 27
Devon's | **CC** 24
Enzo | **CC** 24
Le Grenier | **MV** 23
Le Languedoc | **Nan** 26
L'Étoile | **MV** 26

Pearl	**Nan**	24
Z Red Pheasant	**CC**	27
Ships Inn	**Nan**	24
Sweet/Slice Life	**MV**	25

FRENCH (BISTRO)

| L'Alouette | **CC** | 26 |

ITALIAN

(N=Northern; S=Southern)

Adrian's	**CC**	16
Alberto's	**N**	**CC**	20
Amari	**CC**	22
Buca's Tuscan	**N**	**CC**	23
Casino Wharf	**N**	**CC**	20
Chesca's	**MV**	23
Ciro & Sal's	**N**	**CC**	20
DeMarco	**N**	**Nan**	22
Fanizzi's	**CC**	20
Fazio's	**CC**	20
Z Front St.	**CC**	27
Gina's	**CC**	21
Jetties	**Nan**	14
Jimmy Seas	**MV**	23
La Cucina/Mare	**CC**	25
Lattanzi's	**N**	**MV**	21
Nauset Beach	**N**	**CC**	25
Osteria La Civetta	**N**	**CC**	-
Pi Pizzeria	**S**	**Nan**	23
Sfoglia	**Nan**	24
Siena	**CC**	21

JAPANESE

(* sushi specialist)

Z Inaho*	**CC**	27
Misaki*	**CC**	24
Net Result*	**MV**	25
Sushi by Yoshi*	**Nan**	25

MEDITERRANEAN

Z Abba	**CC**	27
Ardeo	**CC**	20
Blue Moon Bistro	**CC**	24

| **Z** Pisces | **CC** | 27 |
| Trevi Café | **CC** | - |

MEXICAN

| Lorraine's | **CC** | 20 |
| Sharky's | **MV** | 21 |

NEW ENGLAND

Arno's	**Nan**	16
Baxter's	**CC**	18
Capt. Frosty's	**CC**	21
Capt. Parker's	**CC**	18
Chart Room	**CC**	20
Hemisphere	**CC**	17
Home Port	**MV**	20
Jetties	**Nan**	14
Landfall	**CC**	18
Moby Dick's	**CC**	23
Paddock	**CC**	20
Red Inn	**CC**	24
NEW Sidecar Café	**MV**	-

NUEVO LATINO

| Cinco | **Nan** | 26 |

PIZZA

Fairway	**CC**	18
Lattanzi's	**MV**	21
Pi Pizzeria	**Nan**	23

PUB FOOD

| Capt. Kidd | **CC** | 18 |
| Newes/America | **MV** | 18 |

SEAFOOD

Academy Ocean	**CC**	22
Aqua Grille	**CC**	19
Arnold's Lobster	**CC**	23
NEW Atlantic	**MV**	-
Barley Neck Inn	**CC**	20
Baxter's	**CC**	18
Bite	**MV**	26
Bookstore & Rest.	**CC**	19

☑ Brewster Fish | **CC**	26	Roadhouse | **CC**	20
Bubala's | **CC**	16	Ropewalk | **Nan**	-
Capt. Frosty's | **CC**	21	SeaGrille | **Nan**	22
Casino Wharf | **CC**	20	Sir Cricket's | **CC**	24
Catch of the Day | **CC**	25	Straight Wharf | **Nan**	25
Chart Room | **CC**	20	Wicked Oyster | **CC**	24
Cobie's Clam | **CC**	19		

SMALL PLATES

(See also Spanish tapas specialist)

Cooke's | **CC**	-
Dolphin | **CC**	21

Fanizzi's | **CC**	20	Trevi Café | Med. | **CC** —

SOUTH AFRICAN

Fishmonger's | **CC**	18		
Friendly Fisherman | **CC**	24	Karoo Kafe | **CC**	24

SOUTHWESTERN

Home Port | **MV**	20		
Impudent Oyster | **CC**	23	Zapotec | **MV**	19

SPANISH

(* tapas specialist)

JT's Seafood | **CC**	17		
Kate's Seafood | **CC**	20	Cinco* | **Nan**	26
Landfall | **CC**	18	Gracie's Table* | **CC**	23

STEAKHOUSES

Larsen's Fish | **MV**	27		
Liam's | **CC**	20	Roadhouse | **CC**	20

TEAROOMS

Lobster Pot | **CC**	22		
Mac's | **CC**	24	Dunbar Tea | **CC**	22
Marshside | **CC**	15	Optimist Café | **CC**	21

THAI

Moby Dick's | **CC**	23		
Naked Oyster | **CC**	25	☑ Abba | **CC**	27
Nantucket Lobster | **Nan**	19	Alice's | **Nan**	18

Net Result | **MV**	25
Oyster Co. | **CC**	23
Paddock | **CC**	20
☑ Pisces | **CC**	27
Port | **CC**	23

Locations

Includes restaurant names, cuisines and Food ratings.

Cape Cod

BARNSTABLE

Dolphin | *Seafood* 21

BREWSTER

Ardeo | *Med.* 20
🔲 Bramble Inn | *Amer.* 27
🔲 Brewster Fish | *Seafood* 26
🔲 Chillingsworth | *French* 27
Cobie's Clam | *Seafood* 19
JT's Seafood | *Seafood* 17
Kate's Seafood | *Seafood* 20

CATAUMET

Chart Room | *New Eng./Seafood* 20

CHATHAM

Chatham Bars Inn | *Amer.* 22
Chatham Squire | *Eclectic* 18
Impudent Oyster | *Seafood* 23
🔲 Pisces | *Med./Seafood* 27
RooBar | *Amer.* 21
🔲 28 Atlantic | *Amer.* 26
Vining's Bistro | *Eclectic* 24
Wild Goose | *Amer.* 21

COTUIT

Regatta of Cotuit | *Amer.* 25

DENNIS

Blue Moon Bistro | *Med.* 24
Capt. Frosty's | *New Eng./Seafood* 21
Gina's | *Italian* 21
Gracie's Table | *Spanish* 23
Marshside | *Seafood* 15

🔲 Red Pheasant | *Amer./French* 27
Scargo Café | *Amer.* 20

DENNISPORT

Clancy's | *Amer.* 22
Ocean House | *Amer.* 25
Oyster Co. | *Seafood* 23

EASTHAM/ NORTH EASTHAM

Arnold's Lobster | *Seafood* 23
Fairway | *Amer.* 18
Friendly Fisherman | *Seafood* 24
Laura & Tony's | *Amer.* -

EAST ORLEANS/ ORLEANS

🔲 Abba | *Med./Thai* 27
Academy Ocean | *Eclectic/Seafood* 22
Barley Neck Inn | *Amer.* 20
Capt. Linnell | *Amer.* 22
Cooke's | *Seafood* -
Liam's | *Seafood* 20
Nauset Beach | *Italian* 25
Orleans Inn | *Amer.* 17
Sir Cricket's | *Seafood* 24

EAST SANDWICH/ SANDWICH

Amari | *Italian* 22
Aqua Grille | *Amer./Seafood* 19
Bee-Hive Tavern | *Amer.* 19
Belfry Inne | *Amer.* 25
Dan'l Webster | *Amer.* 20
Dunbar Tea | *British/Tearoom* 22
Hemisphere | *Amer.* 17

FALMOUTH/ WEST FALMOUTH

Betsy's Diner	*Diner*	18
Casino Wharf	*Italian/Seafood*	20
Chapoquoit Grill	*Amer.*	22
Coonamessett Inn	*Amer.*	18
Firefly Woodfire	*Eclectic*	20
La Cucina/Mare	*Italian*	25
Laureen's	*Eclectic*	23
Osteria La Civetta	*Italian*	-
RooBar	*Amer.*	21

HARWICH

Buca's Tuscan	*Italian*	23

HARWICH PORT

Cape Sea Grille	*Amer.*	26
Circadia Bistro	*Amer.*	23
L'Alouette	*French*	26
Port	*Amer./Seafood*	23

HYANNIS

Alberto's	*Italian*	20
Ardeo	*Med.*	20
Baxter's	*New Eng./Seafood*	18
Brazilian Grill	*Brazilian*	21
Cooke's	*Seafood*	-
Fazio's	*Italian*	20
HannaH's Fusion	*Asian Fusion*	24
Island Merchant	*Amer./Carib.*	-
Misaki	*Japanese*	24
Naked Oyster	*Seafood*	25
☑ Not Average Joe's	*Amer.*	18
Paddock	*New Eng./Seafood*	20
Roadhouse	*Seafood/Steak*	20

MASHPEE

Bleu	*French*	25
Cooke's	*Seafood*	-
Heather	*Amer.*	-
Siena	*Italian*	21
Trevi Café	*Med.*	-

NORTH TRURO

Adrian's	*Amer./Italian*	16
Terra Luna	*Amer.*	24

OSTERVILLE

Five Bays Bistro	*Amer.*	25

POCASSET

Stir Crazy	*Cambodian*	23

PROVINCETOWN

Bayside Betsy's	*Amer.*	15
Bistro/Crowne Pointe	*Amer.*	22
Bubala's	*Eclectic/Seafood*	16
Cafe Edwige/at Night	*Amer.*	26
Ciro & Sal's	*Italian*	20
Devon's	*Amer./French*	24
Enzo	*French*	24
Fanizzi's	*Amer./Italian*	20
☑ Front St.	*Continental/Italian*	27
Karoo Kafe	*S African*	24
Lobster Pot	*Eclectic/Seafood*	22
Lorraine's	*Mex.*	20
Mews	*Amer.*	27
Napi's	*Eclectic*	19
Post Office	*Amer.*	16
Red Inn	*New Eng.*	24
Ross' Grill	*Amer.*	22

SOUTH YARMOUTH/ YARMOUTH PORT

Anthony Cummaquid	*Continental*	18
Ardeo	*Med.*	20
☑ Inaho	*Japanese*	27
Optimist Café	*Amer./British*	21

TRURO

NEW Blackfish	*Amer.*	24
Whitman House	*Amer.*	21

WELLFLEET

Bookstore & Rest.	*Seafood*	19
Catch of the Day	*Seafood*	25

Menus, photos, voting and more - free at ZAGAT.com

Finely JP's	_Amer._	21
Mac's	_Seafood_	24
Moby Dick's	_New Eng./Seafood_	23
Wicked Oyster	_Amer./Seafood_	24
Winslow's Tavern	_Amer._	20

WEST YARMOUTH

| Capt. Parker's | _New Eng._ | 18 |

WOODS HOLE

Capt. Kidd	_Pub_	18
Fishmonger's	_Amer./Seafood_	18
Landfall	_Seafood_	18

Martha's Vineyard

AQUINNAH

| ☑ Outermost Inn | _Amer._ | 25 |

CHILMARK

| Theo's | _Amer._ | 24 |

EDGARTOWN

Alchemy	_Amer._	22
NEW Atlantic	_Seafood_	-
Atria	_Amer._	25
Chesca's	_Eclectic/Italian_	23
David Ryan's	_Amer._	15
☑ Détente	_Amer._	27
Lattanzi's	_Italian_	21
L'Étoile	_French_	26
Lure	_Amer._	21
Newes/America	_Pub_	18
Sharky's	_Mex._	21
NEW Water St.	_Eclectic_	-

MENEMSHA

Beach Plum	_Amer._	25
Bite	_Seafood_	26
Home Port	_New Eng./Seafood_	20
Larsen's Fish	_Seafood_	27

OAK BLUFFS

Balance	_Amer._	23
Jimmy Seas	_Italian_	23
Lola's	_Cajun/Creole_	22
Offshore Ale	_Amer._	20
Park Corner	_Amer._	22
Sharky's	_Mex._	21
NEW Sidecar Café	_New Eng._	-
Sweet/Slice Life	_Amer._	-
Sweet/Slice Life	_Amer._	25
Zapotec	_SW_	19

VINEYARD HAVEN

Art Cliff Diner	_Diner_	24
☑ Black Dog Tavern	_Amer._	19
Le Grenier	_French_	23
Net Result	_Seafood_	25
NEW Salt Water	_Eclectic_	-
NEW Waterside Mkt.	_Amer._	-
Zephrus	_Amer._	20

WEST TISBURY

| Lambert's Cove | _Amer._ | 25 |

Nantucket

NANTUCKET

Alice's	_Amer./Thai_	18
American Seasons	_Amer._	25
Arno's	_Amer._	16
Black-Eyed Susan's	_Amer._	26
Boarding Hse.	_Amer._	21
Brant Point	_Amer._	21
Brotherhood/Thieves	_Amer._	18
Cambridge St.	_Eclectic_	-
Centre St. Bistro	_Amer._	16
Cinco	_Nuevo Latino_	26
Cioppino's	_Amer._	19
Club Car	_Continental_	20
☑ Company/Cauldron	_Amer._	28
DeMarco	_Italian_	22

LOCATIONS

Even Keel	*Amer.*	19
Fifty-Six Union	*Eclectic*	22
Fog Island	*Amer.*	21
Z Galley Beach	*Eclectic*	24
Jetties	*Italian/New Eng.*	14
Le Languedoc	*French*	26
Lo La 41°	*Eclectic*	21
Nantucket Lobster	*Seafood*	19
Òran Mór	*Eclectic*	24
Pearl	*Asian Fusion/French*	24
Pi Pizzeria	*Pizza*	23
Queequeg's	*Eclectic*	25
Ropewalk	*Seafood*	-

SeaGrille	*Seafood*	22
Sfoglia	*Italian*	24
Ships Inn	*Calif./French*	24
Slip 14	*Amer.*	18
Straight Wharf	*Seafood*	25
Sushi by Yoshi	*Japanese*	25
Z Topper's	*Amer.*	27
29 Fair St.	*Continental*	22
Z 21 Federal	*Amer.*	24

SIASCONSET

Chanticleer	*French*	25
Sconset Café	*Amer.*	21
Summer House	*Amer.*	20